SHATTERED

God's view through
life's broken windows

Rachel & Tim Wright

'My days have passed, my plans are shattered.
Yet the desires of my heart
turn night into day;
in the face of the darkness light is near.'

Job 17:11–12

To our amazing children Sam, Jonah and Ethan.

We are mostly shattered because of you three,
but wouldn't have it any other way.

Published 2019 by CWR, Waverley Abbey House, Waverley Lane, Farnham, Surrey
GU9 8EP, UK. CWR is a Registered Charity – Number 294387 and a Limited Company
registered in England – Registration Number 1990308.

For a list of National Distributors, visit cwr.org.uk/distributors

Concept development, editing, design and production by CWR.
Every effort has been made to ensure that this book contains the correct permissions
and references, but if anything has been inadvertently overlooked the Publisher will be
pleased to make the necessary arrangements at the first opportunity. Please contact the
Publisher directly.
Cover image: adobestock/Ollirod
Back cover photo: Krula Photography
Printed in the UK by Page Bros
ISBN: 978-1-78259-896-1

ABOUT THE AUTHORS

Tim

Many of Tim's best friends are trees, although he talks to real people too. He is a thinker, worker, drummer, husband, part-time GP and full-time dad of three boys. He tends to stop to look closely at small things on his way, despite being pathologically averse to arriving late.

He loves peanut butter and liquorish but not necessarily at the same time. He hates plans being changed at short notice but paradoxically would love to be more spontaneous. Like many men, he attempts to bury his scars but fails spectacularly as they rise to the surface uninvited. Regardless of his fear of failure, he fails often, resulting in a tendency to become quite fearful.

He feels closest to God when managing a small woodland in Kent. When he stretches up like the trees to the heavens, God always seems just out of reach, even if he's on his tiptoes. Tim plans to keep on reaching up though.

Rachel

Rachel spends her life moving discarded objects back to where they belong. She is a nurse, writer, speaker, trainer and mum of three sons, one of whom has severe disabilities and life-limiting epilepsy. Despite her guilt, she gets a lot of help because she isn't Superwoman (just don't tell the children).

As well as laundry and endlessly tidying toys, she blogs at bornattherighttime.com for which she won a BAPs award for Blogger 'Making a Difference' in 2018. In 2015, she published her memoir, *The Skies I'm Under*. She believes an enjoyable evening includes a good book or romantic comedy and a glass of gin with lots of ice. Occasionally, she makes herself go for a run to counteract her love of salt and vinegar crisps.

In lots of small ways, she tries to save the planet and is passionate about bringing a faith perspective to life's brokenness. She is challenged daily that God can often be found where she least expects Him.

CONTENTS

WHY YOU SHOULD READ THIS BOOK

'While being aware that a book like *Shattered* might help me, I'd rather sit on a fork than admit it. This isn't my kind of book. If I hadn't written much of it, I probably wouldn't pick it off the shelf. I'd like to complain that I'm not well served in the 'Christian devotional' genre, but it's more likely that I am simply very bad at serving myself. I'm sure there are many people (perhaps many of whom are men) who feel the same way.

That said, I think *Shattered* is different. It is the distillation of a decade of grappling with big issues such as suffering, anxiety, disappointment and hope. I believe this book has something new to reveal to everyone, even people like me. So, go on, take a little serving of *Shattered* – what's the worst that could happen?'
Tim Wright, Co-Author of *Shattered*, shamelessly plugging his own book

'Refreshingly honest and vulnerable. More than just a devotional, *Shattered* challenges us to recognise God with us, even in our very darkest moments.'
Rob Parsons OBE, Author, Speaker, Chief Executive of Care for the Family

'Offering grace, love and comfort, this book of devotionals is a brilliant resource for anyone going through hard times.'
Pete and Sammy Greig, Leaders of Emmaus Road Church, Guildford

'We live in a hurting world, yet we're often led to paper over the cracks; to present a life in which our struggles are hidden behind an illusion of what we're told we should be. What if we said no? What if we dared to stop hiding? What if we had the courage to live broken?

Rachel and Tim Wright are honest and real. By sharing their own brokenness, they encourage us in ours, even when it's hard. They help us acknowledge our pain – to ourselves and to God – and, in doing so, we discover that 'broken' doesn't always need fixing. 'Broken' has a beauty beyond anything we imagined.'
Emily Owen, Author and Speaker

'*Shattered* is one of the richest devotional books I have ever read. It's easy sometimes to give a book a genre title like 'devotional' and then have a kind of picture in mind for how you imagine it will be. Well, *Shattered* breaks through all those pre-conceptions. It doesn't follow a traditional pattern and is actually a glorious mix of Bible teaching, autobiographical snippets, uplifting reflections and meditations, suggested further readings and amazing spiritual exercises using the most ordinary of things. The glue that holds it all together is authenticity. The whole book is full of it; the authenticity of Rachel and Tim's own heartbreak, struggles, pain and humour plus the stories of others going through their own shattering traumas.

Unlike the usual 'page a day' devotional format, *Shattered* invites you to look the through different windows of the struggles we experience in life, and to recognise God's loving presence with us as we gaze. Rachel and Tim write from their own perspectives and invite us to discover the God who is with us in our heartbreak, who weeps when we weep and rejoices when we rejoice, and somehow miraculously enables us to grow from the ashes with a new beauty and strength.

You don't have to be going through trauma to find this book enriching. But if you have or still are, then I fully believe *Shattered* will help you walk your journey with more hope, more comfort and the certainty of God's love always with you. I have no hesitation in recommending *Shattered* to all.'
Tracy Williamson, Author and Speaker, Marilyn Baker Ministries

'This book is completely amazing! I don't think I've ever read anything that is so 'real'. As the parent of an autistic son with epilepsy, the writing hits me with total honesty and authenticity. I absolutely melted over the idea of learning to be content with the skies you are under. More than a powerful message, Rachel and Tim's deeply affecting words feel like a direction; a goal; a path to follow. It's incredible that they are able to express the reality of their lives so eloquently and with such hope and vision.'
Alexa Tewkesbury, Author

'A moving and sensitive book, which offers encouragement without papering over the cracks, and reminds us that even though life can be messy, painful and chaotic, love, light and faith are always to be found.'
Rev Kate Bottley, Priest and Media Presenter

'I have had the pleasure of getting to know Rachel and Tim over the last couple of years, and I find them inspirational not only in the way they write and talk but in the way they live. For me, integrity is one of the most attractive values. What I love about this book is that it's honest and real, and shows how God meets us in the everyday moments of our lives, especially in the hard times.'
Patrick Regan OBE, Author and Speaker, Chief Executive of Kintsugi Hope

HOW TO USE THIS BOOK

This isn't the same as other devotionals. You aren't expected to read every day. There are many pressures in life. Sometimes it is hard and overwhelming. However life feels for you right now, let this be a safe place. If you manage to sit down with a cup of tea, that's good. God can meet you there, He's waiting. Some days, the only moment you get to yourself is while sitting on a toilet. You take what you can.

- Instead of 'days', each section is called a window. There are 40 windows to look through. There are no rules regarding how long you spend on each window or when to move on to the next view. Each window includes a short verse from the Bible and a reference to a longer passage. (These will be quoted from the New International Version unless otherwise stated.) Sometimes the focus verse is from the longer chunk of reading – sometimes it's from a different bit of the Bible.

- Every window varies slightly in length and topic. Each one has a reflection. Some will have practical elements while others provide space for you to write, draw, or fill something in. Don't be afraid to write in this book – it's yours, and it's up to you how much you engage with each window.

- Some meditations have additional content available online, indicated with this icon: ▼▣ . These can be read or listened to free through the Shattered website (shattered.org.uk), where you will also find links to songs and videos we refer to.

- The only thing we ask you to do at each window is stop. A moment of silence can go a long way.

- As well as telling you more about our view of life, some of our friends have written their own stories, giving different perspectives. We believe our life stories are the heartbeat of God on earth. Not just the 'good' bits; especially the 'not-good' bits. If you are like Rachel you will devour each story right at the beginning. If you are like Tim you may not read every one and may try to avoid any that are too close to home.

- Finally, if you can do this with someone else, do. Maybe find someone at church, a friend, partner, or someone on our Facebook page. Create a WhatsApp group, text or call, make connections that mean you are not walking this path alone.
- We have written this devotional together and so for clarity we have identified whose voice is speaking in each window.

Our prayer:

As you take in the view, we pray you will know you are not alone. We pray that you will receive hope and peace amidst the light and darkness of each day. We pray you will feel less shattered as you see God's view through life's broken windows.

THE VIEW AS THE PARENTS OF A DISABLED CHILD
Our story – Rachel

'Any movements?' asked the midwife as I lay on a hospital bed with a monitor strapped to my rotund stomach, the sound of my baby's heartbeat thumping through the air.

'No, afraid not,' I replied. Suddenly her tone changed and I was told the doctor would be with me in a minute.

After a short consultation, the doctor made it clear she wanted to deliver my baby straightaway. Tim (also a doctor – I'm a nurse) was working on a nearby ward, and as he arrived we were shown to a more sterile room on the labour ward. The doctor reassured us that all the clinical signs so far were good, but the safest option was to deliver our baby soon.

This wasn't the plan.

Much of my pregnancy hadn't met my expectations, but mostly in pretty trivial ways. I wasn't the maternal goddess I had imagined, prancing around with flowers in my hair feeling beautiful, glowing and whole. Instead I developed the ability to vomit surreptitiously in car parks around Essex while what felt like an alien squirmed around in my stomach. To finish it off, I had been sorely disappointed when my waters didn't break while I was out shopping in Boots – despite all the jumping up and down I did in the laxative aisle. So I never was awarded that big bag of baby goodies the urban myth had promised me had my membranes ruptured on cue.

But this was different. Although everyone remained calm and jovial, everything started happening very quickly.

Before long, my legs were lifted onto the trolley, fizzing and tingling as though they belonged to someone else. In theatre, Tim sat by my head, averting his eyes from all that was happening to the lower part my body. As a doctor, it seems that cutting people open is absolutely fine until it is your wife, and then it becomes distinctly less acceptable.

The hustle and bustle of theatre continued. The chatter of the obstetrician and midwives was accompanied by the clatter of instruments and trolleys. Everything remained un-rushed and light-hearted. Then, just after 2pm on Wednesday 12 October 2005, a slimy, limp baby was removed from my womb with the exclamation from the delivering doctor that we had a boy.

Within a few moments, however, I became concerned that I couldn't hear my son cry and sent Tim to investigate. As he took the long, slow steps back across the theatre, he considered his words and gently lowered his head.

'He isn't breathing.' Tim's gaze penetrated my heart. 'The doctors are trying to resuscitate him now.'

A kiss on my forehead sealed his words. I insisted he go back and watch over our son. So Tim retraced his steps, passing familiar equipment and suddenly sullen faces. The anaesthetist behind me touched my shoulder as I silently wept. Despite being unable to feel most of my body, the pain was overwhelming.

Medical staff started buzzing around and after several minutes I momentarily saw the top of my son's head, which I was encouraged to kiss before he was whisked off to the neonatal intensive care unit to be ventilated. Then the sobbing really began, interrupting the uncomfortable hush that engulfed the theatre.

Everything had changed.

As our son precariously lingered on the brink of life and death, we knew he needed a name, and fast. We liked the idea of a family name; it certainly saved us the effort of being original. Then, when we saw our newborn with his bald head and rim of dark hair around the sides it made us think of my dad.

Dad is a remarkable, godly man, full of humility and grace. He has a soft Irish accent nurtured on the streets of Belfast and his name is… Norman. Sadly, we aren't cool enough to get away with a name like that, but fortunately Dad's middle name is Samuel, after his father. When we discovered Samuel means 'God hears', it seemed the perfect fit; we really needed our prayers to be heard.

And it seemed they were.

At 12 days old, on no medication, Sammy was discharged from hospital. Clutching an appointment card for an MRI scan in ten weeks' time, we took our miracle baby home. For little over two months we were thrust into the chaos of being first-time parents. We soon discovered that babies need more equipment for a trip to the supermarket than we previously needed trekking across New Zealand. Breast pads and nappies littered our bedroom as we bravely fought against the midnight tide of poo and puke.

Then the day of the MRI arrived.

After a long, slow walk down monotonous hospital corridors, we were shown into a small room where the doctor introduced herself. Gently and carefully, she explained that it wasn't good news. The MRI showed severe brain damage. Her words were spoken lightly, yet the room began to close in. With soft and meticulous explanations, she described in detail how the scan showed Sam had been 'very unlucky'.

I sat rigid and gazed across the room. She explained that Sammy's brain damage was both unusual and extensive. Her words became a blur of white noise as my mind drowned out the truth, replaying all the times I may have allowed this catastrophic event to occur.

How had I missed my baby struggling inside me?

What kind of mother was I?

The doctor continued to explain that Sammy would have complex disabilities. Tim bravely asked questions, and I was surprised at his ability to talk with a steady voice. The doctor remained vague. We weren't told he would never walk, talk or eat, but we were told nothing could be taken for granted. It was as though the doctor had erased the vibrant wall of our hopes and dreams with a paintbrush dripping with brilliant white paint, leaving our future void and unknown.

Through the quiet, careful words of a consultant, a bomb had exploded in the middle of our lives, splintering our world into thousands of tiny pieces. Like walking wounded, we staggered out of the hospital holding on to each other, dazed and bewildered. The words spoken over us rang in our ears. As reality began to sink in, I was surprised at the magnitude of my shock. I simply hadn't prepared myself for hearing that my little boy had profound brain damage.

Over a decade later, the memory of this time can be conjured up by simply washing my hands with hospital soap or the faint beep of a monitor. Our trinket box of flashbacks has been somewhat extended since those first few weeks to include helicopter flights to an ITU (in France), life-threatening seizures, Tim performing CPR on his knees on our bathroom floor, being told never to feed our son, and various operations. But each one is counteracted with laughter and joy, tenderness and hope, and the fact that light really does have the power to outshine darkness.

Our life today isn't easy. It is consumed with the complexity of 24-hour care and the reality that our son is unlikely to live to adulthood. But with it comes a vulnerability and appreciation for living that is only nurtured by our knowing we all live a broken and yet incredibly beautiful life.

Your story

(Rachel)

'Come, see a man who told me everything I've ever done.'
(John 4:29)

If you have the time: **John 4:4–29**

'I used to be addicted to drugs and alcohol but now I'm living as a missionary in Peru saving hundreds of people for Christ.'*

I'm a sucker for happy endings. While sitting in church I lean forward, poised and green with envy as a remarkable testimony brings people from weeping to whooping in celebration.

As a much-loved middle child of five, who grew up in a western, Christian home, I didn't have a rough start. I'm a Miss Goodie-Two-Shoes who failed to have the courage for a single drag of a cigarette, never mind any significant level of rebellion. I wanted to be the one with a story of beating the odds, struggling and striving, being lost and then miraculously found. I longed for a tale that told of redemption from my once downtrodden life into something extraordinary. Without such a tale, my story felt insignificant.

But that was a lie. My story matters. God's story in me matters – even without the Hollywood ending.

Since I have started sharing our story with people publicly, I have employed the use of a story bracelet to help every person see they have a story. A story that counts. It might sound a bit *Blue Peter*, but using a length of thread and bowl full of beads, a person gets to pause and look back over their story to date. Using different colours, designs and shapes, each bead represents a momentous event or relationship. Once finished, the bracelet depicts the highs and lows of the journey so far. This may not sound appealing if you're not a 'beads and string' kind of person, but it's surprising how even the toughest of us end up fighting over the 'best' beads.

It is an activity adapted from the *Essence* course by Rob Frost, which is simple yet challenging and fuels fun, deep and thoughtful conversations. People open up about the parts of life that stand out and how they should be portrayed. I have sat alongside a woman as she searched for beads that would adequately represent the pain of her miscarriages, and another hunting for a bead for the TV show *Love Island*… each to their own. It feels much easier to share the moments of life woven together to create our story while hunting around in a bowl of beads. There is something about not looking into each other's eyes that gives us the confidence to be more vulnerable.

The truth is, we all have a story. We have a life full of joys and losses, highs and lows. One of the first steps in dealing with difficult times is to reflect and acknowledge the steps we've taken so far. When we recognise what brought us here, we can be reminded of the times when God has sustained us; the times we've felt held by loved ones, supported and nurtured. We get the chance to remember the good times that seem painfully out of reach while sitting in the gloom of our current difficulties. But we also need to allow ourselves to acknowledge when we felt isolated, alone, rejected: it means we can identify the struggles and trials that have shaped us.

Think about the woman at the well in John's Gospel (John 4). Despite her colourful past, being known by Jesus brought her comfort, not shame. Jesus saw her as she really was, and although her story was told, she was left with the fragrance of hope and not the taste of condemnation. It is only by acknowledging where we have been and what has shaped us that we can courageously take the next step along life's path. I love how Brené Brown puts it: 'Rumbling with our story and owning our truth in order to write a new, more courageous ending transforms who we are and how we engage with the world.'[1]

*Not really anyone's testimony.

TEABAG MEDITATION

Pour yourself (or make someone else) a cup of tea.
   But let's do this slowly.
   Take time over each step.
   While the kettle is boiling, pick up a teabag and feel the dry, brown leaves between your fingers.
   Can you smell the tea?
   Imagine those luscious, green leaves reaching towards the sun in a faraway place. Picture the thick, waxy foliage of the tea plant catching the drenching rain before drips spill over, falling to the

rich, brown earth. Life-giving water seeps into the soil, nourishing expectant roots. Then the midday sun beats down, oppressive and relentless, yet the perfect companion for growth.

Imagine the leaves being ripped off the plant and haphazardly discarded into a bag; the greenery scorched, browned, dried up and then crushed; the shrivelled, lifeless plant packaged into dark containers and transported thousands of miles.

Notice the water boiling and steam beginning to rise.

Put the bag in your cup and pour the boiling water over it.

See, smell and watch the dried leaves infuse life into the scalding water. Notice the swirling flavours long trapped inside, dormant in the leaves for months and miles.

Hold the cup. Soak up the warmth in your hands and the steam in your face. So much has happened to bring you to this moment.

Consider your life story. The sun, the rain, the twists and turns. Your story is much more interesting and much more important than a teabag.

Defining moments

(Tim)

'Sooner or later bad luck hits us all.'
(Ecclesiastes 9:11, *The Message*)

If you have the time: Ecclesiastes 9:7–12

What a fantastic verse from Ecclesiastes to brighten your day.

OK, so you won't see that verse printed beneath a sunset on a bookmark in your local Christian bookshop. It can, however, be deeply reassuring to those of us who feel that we are experiencing some of life's 'bad luck'. It's comforting if you feel you're not the only one. I personally am encouraged that the Bible acknowledges bad stuff happens to good people; to all people.

Everyone lives through defining moments. For some, it might be a single event, but for many it is a cascade of events – a series of decisions and experiences that create a domino effect leading us into unknown and often unwanted territory. These moments shape us, whether we like it or not.

For those of us who have children, we know that the birth

of our first child is a defining moment. From then on life is either BC (Before Children) or AD (Another Day without enough sleep). It is a defining moment, and everything before or after is then viewed in relation to the changes that occur.

When Sam was born, it was as though a permanent line had been etched into the sand of my life, an indelible mark resistant to waves or tide. This mark would be a pivot for the rest of our lives; a before and after defining moment.

As I sit in my consultation room at work, I recognise the significant lines in the sand I draw with my patients. I try to craft my words carefully when I know a moment will be remembered. I have sat with patients recently diagnosed with cancer, dementia or miscarriage. The air is thick with emotions and questions without answers.

Some live with the struggle of repeated negative pregnancy tests, which causes them to weep in the bathroom and undergo intrusive investigations. For others, divorce papers, a redundancy letter or university rejection land heavy on their doormat leading to a spiral of stress, difficult to navigate.

I have patients who live in abusive relationships, challenging domestic situations and many other stressful surroundings that spark insurmountable feelings of anxiety and depression. And then there are others still who suffer under the grief of the untimely and unexpected death of a loved one, which breaks their hearts and changes their lives forever.

The question is not *if* but rather *when* will we suffer loss or disappointment. It can be tempting to try to measure the severity of our loss. We look at others and try to decide if our lives are harder, or better. We try to quantify our grief or the magnitude of our tragedy, but these measurements are arbitrary and unhelpful.

When an event feels like it defines you and splits your life into 'before' and 'after', take hope from knowing that although these moments shape us, they don't define us. Our identity remains in God throughout the momentous events in our life. He sees the bigger picture through our life's broken windows.

Consider the defining moments of your life, the good and not-so-good, which created a before and after. Write a list here to reflect on:

_____

_____

_____

_____

_____

_____

_____

_____

_____

_____

_____

Pebbles

(Tim)

'The earth takes shape like clay under a seal:
its features stand out like those of a garment.' (Job 38:14)

If you have the time: 2 Corinthians 4:7–18

Go and find a pebble.

Go on. We aren't going any further until you have a pebble.

Take a minute, a day, a week – but work out how you are
going to get a pebble in your hand. Ask for help if you need to,
and then come back.

PEBBLE MEDITATION

Find a quiet place. Stop, listen and reflect.

Pick up your pebble.

It is like you in some ways – just another pebble
among many from the beach, or your garden, yet it
is unique.

Turn it over in your hand.

Study every detail.

Now hold it tight.

Imagine that you are that pebble...

Long ago, you began to form. At the beginning of time, you began. And through the minutes and the hours and the years you were carefully shaped.

First there was darkness. All you knew was fire in the earth. But slowly the earth cooled and the fire was soothed by the waters.

The sands began to settle. Particles came together with pressure and time, and as layer formed upon layer, liquids crystallised.

And the darkness slowly lifted, and gave way to light as you tumbled from the cliff edge into the rolling sea.

Now, here you are, lying on the surface in the warmth of the sunshine. The waves of the sea pick you up and churn you over, crashing rock against rock, the rolling sands shifting and sifting. Some of your sharp edges are smoothed and polished by the constant movement, tumbling along the seabed, exposed on the beach until another wave drags you up shore.

At times, the crashing chips your edges, exposing smooth rock, and again the waves batter you.

Parts are smooth and polished; some are more rough and coarse, at least on the outside. Some are beautiful; others look plainer with beautiful hidden details, or their beauty is only apparent on closer inspection.

Each pebble has been shaped by the pressure, the fire, the waves and the lifting movement of rhythmic sea.

Your shape, your form, both hidden and exposed have created your beauty; made you who you are today. Your story has shaped you and your smooth surface and weathered edges are unique gifts that can be shared and celebrated.

This is your story.

And you became yourself – lovingly shaped by the gentle, deliberate power of the rain and wind and waves, and by the slow, unstoppable movement of the earth.

All pebbles show one face, but hide what is inside them: the cracks; the crystals; the hard heart; the bright colours.

But God sees you.

God chooses you.

He chooses His children – as they are.

He picks you up and holds you close.

God has you and your story in His hands.

The pressure; the waves; the smoothing and the breaking.

All of it is in His hands.

All of you is His.

Treasure

(Tim)

*'In the beginning you laid the foundations of the earth,
and the heavens are the work of your hands.'* (Psalm 102:25)

If you have the time: Psalm 139:13–24

We are fortunate to live by the sea. A ten-minute walk with three children and a wheelchair in tow, and we breathe in the salty sea air as we reach the muddy plains of the Thames estuary. Here the kids like to gather 'treasures' from the beach. These precious finds include stones, shells, crab claws, and the occasional bit of pottery from an imagined sunken pirate ship.

Like our last reflection, the treasures we gather have been battered, worn and ground smooth by waves over the years. The same is true of us. We bear the scars, the marks and the crystallised beauty left by the ebb and flow, the joys and sorrows of life. These are the experiences that make us who we are and shape our identity.

Maybe you feel your body or mind is broken; perhaps you are disappointed by the dizzy fragility of our human frame.

You may have found that bits of you don't work like they're supposed to, or didn't work all that well from the start. We tend to try to hide our brokenness and cover up our blemishes to present a more sanitised, pure, acceptable identity. We want people to see us as whole, productive, purposeful and valuable. We feel anger and resentment at a body and mind that fails to be what we hope or need. Yet this is the body and mind you have – the one God gave you. Being at peace with it, and loving it, is necessary in loving God and others. Maybe God has physical healing in store for your future – maybe not – but at this time and in this place, you can still love your body and be kind to your spirit. In every circumstance, we can say:

> *'I thank you, High God—you're breathtaking!*
> *Body and soul, I am marvelously made!*
> *I worship in adoration—what a creation!'*
> **Psalm 139:13–14 (*The Message*)**

I am currently subjected daily to the music and lyrics of *The Greatest Showman*.[2] It's a film Rachel loves and she has managed to brainwash our children with her passion. Before Sam is collected for school in the morning, Rachel and the boys are often found singing and prancing around the kitchen to the now iconic track *This is Me*. The song is a proclamation of no longer being left in the dark, not hiding our brokenness, but with boldness and great fanfare declaring, 'I am brave, I am bruised, I am who I'm meant to be: this is me.'

When I'm walking home from the beach with my children's pockets bulging with treasures they couldn't bear to leave behind, I am reminded of God's love for us *and* our brokenness. Our identity is in God, and He is not simply interested in 'the good bits'. He treasures our broken and worn out bits just as much.

We need to stop and remember that we are treasures in the hands of God. He has scooped us up with our cracks and chips. He holds us, and even when others might pass us by without a glance, He says, 'You are mine. You are treasured.'

MIRROR MEDITATION

Dare to look in the mirror.

Take in the image of you, exactly as you are: perfectly imperfect.

Is there a part of your body that does not 'work' as you hoped? Consider it tenderly, lovingly. You are fearfully and wonderfully made.

Do you feel your mind and emotions falter and fail you?

Take a moment to see the beauty in a fragile, sensitive and vulnerable soul.

Take in the grey hairs, bumps, scars and blemishes. Each wrinkle is a souvenir of your journey. Every laugh, every smile and every tear shed has left its mark. See the beauty in it; see the beauty in you.

Look into your own eyes and see the Spirit of God residing in you. See His craftsmanship and His love.

Your identity is not in what you earn, your strength, your intelligence, or your attractiveness. It is in being a purposefully designed and created child of God.

You are a much-loved treasure.

THE VIEW OF LIFE WITH MENTAL HEALTH ISSUES
Jay's story

For the last few years I have mostly been a diagnosis:

'Severe clinical depression, with a side serving of generalised anxiety disorder.'

At times, it has felt as though there was no *Me*.

A few years of chronic pain triggered a severe deterioration in my mental health, resulting in five years oscillating between various medications (Citalopram, Sertraline and Prozac – all of them horrible), with some drug-free spells along the way. Of course, the chronic pain was not the sole cause – it was one of a handful. But whatever else was in the mix brought to the surface 30 years of insecurities, confidence and self-esteem issues. For three decades I'd been hiding behind a mask of alcohol and denial.

Despite many physiotherapists, counsellors and Google searches, I was still confused. Everything was about getting me back to normal. But what is normal?

Along the way, I've met many people with similar (but always different) issues. Many bad days (interspersed with some good days) later, I've started to realise that there is no 'normal' – we are all different and truly unique.

Only when I started to be more open and accepting, or allow myself to be vulnerable in any way, did I realise that there were some positives to come out of my experience. I'm not the old me – I'm not even sure who the old me was, I'd built up so much of a facade. Part of this was because of my own internal problems, and part of it was trying to conform to what society expected of me. Thankfully I've now worked through a lot of this.

Although it's not easy, I can usually get through the bad days and recognise that they do pass. I'm also more thankful for the small but enjoyable things in life. The main lesson I've learned is that I am simply me, and that my depression and anxiety are just small parts of that.

Jay Greasley

Detour

(Rachel)

'Father, if you are willing, take this cup from me; yet not my will, but yours be done.' (Luke 22:42)

If you have the time: **Ruth 1:3–18**

There aren't many parts of our marriage that are defined as 'blue' or 'pink', but driving the car through unknown country lanes is something that very definitely gives us clear roles. We have discovered that the best way to avoid an argument is for me to drive, and Tim to direct. Even with the advent of satnav, we still require a living, breathing navigator in our car. Sometimes there are lots of 'lefts' to bear and it isn't totally clear (at least to Tim) which one we should actually take. (That and the fact that Tim doesn't like having the satnav audio on – maybe the insightful direction of just one woman is enough.)

There are different theories as to why our particular driving routine works. It might be because Tim needs three years, four months and 21 days' notice before turning off a road. It may be because if I'm directing, I get distracted on my phone and don't mention the turning until it can only be seen in the rearview mirror. Either way, me driving with Tim navigating works best.

But since we have the benefit of live, electronic maps telling us what the traffic is doing, occasionally we need to take an alternative route. Even though the road ahead looks perfectly clear, the red and orange streaks on the map indicate we are better off going in another direction before we end up in a traffic jam. In travelling terms, this is called a detour – when we need to adjust our expected route and go another way.

But it isn't the same when Tim and I go for a jog. On the rare occasion that we get to run together somewhere new, we grab a map to plan our route. Suddenly we aren't interested in the fastest and most direct option. Instead we want to find the woods to run through, the lake to run alongside, or hill to ascend and enjoy the view. It is the varying terrain that makes the run enjoyable. Although my vote tends to favour 'flat and easy', we usually head for 'hilly, rugged and challenging'.

Two very dear friends of ours have had to take a harrowing detour in recent years. When their neighbourhood was bombed in Daraa, Syria, they left with three young boys and searched for safety. Crossing the border to Jordan, my friend carried her severely disabled son in her arms for the duration of the one-week walk. Alongside, her husband carried their other children and whatever belongings they had salvaged. For a week, they slowly trudged along a sun-scorched, dusty roadside with little food and water. Today they live down our street and we are privileged to call them friends, but their grateful hearts will always be broken for the loved ones they may never see again and a devastated country they miss. In comparison, the deviation in my life can feel insignificant but

I am inspired by how our friends live. Yes, they are not where they want to be. War, death and bombs shattered their life plans but they live as though their unexpected route wasn't simply a detour, but a journey in its own right.

We might find ourselves thrust on an alternative road for reasons we would normally choose to avoid, but when it comes to being alive what matters is the journey – where it takes us, and what we learn along the way. It doesn't make sense that finding the easiest, fastest and shortest road through life to death or heaven is the best option.

I'm not very quick off the blocks, so this realisation came years after Sam was born. It came slowly and unsuspectingly. Like a sun rising into the dawn I started seeing the journey and its unsuspecting transformation as the essence of life. It isn't about avoiding the pitfalls of suffering and pain. When I came to see life as a journey and not just a detour, I learned to love the skies I was under.

Think of a journey you make regularly.

Do you always take the quickest, most efficient route?

It may be your journey to work, or taking the kids to school.

It may be the quickest way to get to the shops.

Next time, take a detour.

Take in a hill or a view, try to walk through the park or go via a friend's house. Make time to remind yourself that life is about the journey, not the destination.

Myths and hope
(Tim)

'And God is faithful; he will not let you be tempted beyond what you can bear.' (1 Corinthians 10:13)

If you have the time: Philippians 1:12–21

'I love it when a plan comes together,' says Hannibal from the A-team as another mission falls into place perfectly and the good guys win the day – again. Wouldn't it be nice, just once, to take the kids to the beach and sum up the whole day by saying, 'I love it when a plan comes together!'* We love things to fall perfectly into place, but outside of 80s TV, we have to deal with the real world where loose ends don't always get tied up and things don't always make sense.

At ten weeks old, an MRI scan confirmed Sam had severe and complex brain damage. By his first birthday, he had been registered blind, was unable to sit or grasp, had to be fed via a tube into his stomach, and was regularly suffering life-threatening seizures.

'God only gives you as much as you can bear'

(1 Corinthians 10:13) and 'everything happens for a reason' (Ecclesiastes 3:1) were both spoken to us as we watched Sam fight for his life. (For more on this topic, I'd recommend Kate Bowler's book, *Everything Happens for a Reason: And Other Lies I've Loved*, which beautifully unravels one woman's struggles with sayings such as these while enduring bowel cancer.) There are some Christian cultures that try to explain every event in terms of an attack or blessing. They say it is either one or the other, and the trick is to find out which one applies.

But life – and God – is not that simple. When we find ourselves in painful and tragic circumstances, it isn't always helpful to imagine a chess-playing God moving us around like pawns, lining us up for some cosmic lesson. There simply isn't a reason for everything that happens (or, at least, that reason remains a stubborn mystery throughout our lives).

Jesus promised us the road would be tough. He didn't dish out get-out-of-jail-free cards to His disciples. He might even have mentioned the need to carry a cross. It wasn't a cross of wealth, health and prosperity, but one like His, which dug into His shoulders and caused Him to stumble.

Yes, God has claimed power over death, but until He comes again we will all experience what it is to die. Yes, God is master and creator of the universe, but devastation still exists all over our broken and fragile world.

Because of Jesus, one thing we know about God is that He is prepared to get dust between His toes as He treads the dirty roads with us. When life in all its guises hurts us, God is there. He has given you your life that you might walk through it, on the earth, at this time, in its current state of brokenness and imperfection with Him. Some things don't make sense. Some things remain a mystery. Sometimes life is hard and heart-breaking. But I refuse to believe in a God who engineers tsunamis, the starvation of communities, 40-year wars and the sexual abuse of young children, just to teach us a lesson.

What is different for those who trust God is that there is absolutely nothing beyond God's power to create life and love from shattered pieces. In every aspect of life – the ordinary, painful, whimsical and tragic – we can recognise the mystery and majesty of God and claim it as holy ground.

History shows us that God has always used the wilderness, the trials and challenges to help us be more like Him – just ask David, Naomi, Esther, Paul or Moses. In every wonderful, miserable, ordinary and remarkable part of life, God is present. Each aspect of our lives is holy and soaked in God's presence if we take notice. As God instructed Moses by the burning bush:

> *'Take off your sandals, for the place where you are standing is holy ground.'*
>
> **Exodus 3:5**

When at the end of the day there is no cigar and plans refuse to come together, we pray that you abandon your need to make sense of things. Instead, take off your sandals. Amidst the pain and mess, God is showing up. He is weeping with you, touching you gently on the shoulder and saying, 'I know it is hard. I am standing here with you on holy ground.'

*Said no father of three, ever.

HIGHER GROUND MEDITATION

Take off your shoes and socks.

Stand if you can.

Place your feet firmly on the ground.

You are standing on holy ground.

Stop.

Breathe.

Feel the texture of the flooring beneath your feet.

Stretch and curl your toes.

Think of the contact between your body and the floor.

Is the floor smooth, coarse, hard or soft?

Are your feet tired and weary, or keen to be on the move?

Feel the world beneath your feet. Stop and consider where you are standing in your life. Acknowledge that wherever you are, in the uncertainty, beauty, mess, discomfort or joy, God is here.

In this time and in this place, God says, 'the place where you are standing is holy ground' (Exodus 3:5).

Seasons
(Tim)

'As long as the earth endures,
seedtime and harvest,
cold and heat,
summer and winter,
day and night
will never cease.' (Genesis 8:22)

If you have the time: Jeremiah 17:5–8

Look at your life. What season are you in, and why?

Don't view it as something you are passing through to get to the next thing, but a season of its own. Each season has its own characteristics, beauty, achievements and hardships.

Spring
Spring begins with very little to see, but subtle changes are all around. Looking past the wintery scene of barren, lifeless twigs, there are buds starting to show. The honeysuckle and elder are first off the blocks.

Finally, the sun begins to bring warmth. New life springs up: vibrant flowers; full, green trees; the air is full of excited bird calls. They demonstrate a promise of abundance and hope for the future. The days are longer. Frequent showers nourish the earth. There is breakthrough and growth.

Spring is a season of quiet joy in the hard-to-find places. There is activity, productivity and fruitfulness.

There is hope for the future in the middle of drenching showers.

Summer

Summer sees things settle a little into the warmth. There is a slowing down. The birds have nested and some, like the cuckoo, think it's time to go already. Others, like the swift, arrive to make the most of the humid air, laden with insects. There is abundance; there is comfort. There is light and time to enjoy the sun perched high in the sky, warming the earth.

The land becomes dry. The once bright green leaves become worn and tired in the late summer heat as growth and activity slow.

Summer is a season of rest and comfort and bright light.

It can also be a season of heat, drought and fatigue.

Autumn

Autumn sees a change in the air as the light fades, almost too fast. The sun dips lower, bringing an inkling that the warmth will soon turn. As the greenery senses the chill of the stretching night, an abundance of fruit arrives.

Berries and apples ripen with a sweetness born from the now fading sun. Mushrooms breathe extravagant new life into a decaying stump. An atmosphere of preparing for the future hangs over the dampening woods. The jay is harvesting and storing acorns, wondering if the cold will bite hard this year.

Autumn is a season of abundance and coming to fruition.

It is a season of anxiety for the future. Of letting things go.

Winter

Winter brings expectations of cold, crisp, blue skies and white-blanketed hills that give way to dark, grey, bitter days. Biting winds whip the last of the leaves from the now dead-looking branches.

Low, heavy skies darken too soon in the day. Night rules over the day with only glimpses of light breaking through. The beauty of sharp frost crystals bristles from every twig, accompanied by the refreshing silence that only a thick blanket of snow can bring.

Winter is a season of loss, of what once was, of hardship and fighting through each day.

It is a season of astounding, fragile beauty, surpassing all other seasons, seen only when you dare brave the frozen air.

What season are you in, and why?

_____

_____

_____

_____

_____

Holly and ivy
(Tim)

'Be patient, then, brothers and sisters, until the Lord's coming. See how the farmer waits for the land to yield its valuable crop, patiently waiting for the autumn and spring rains.' (James 5:7)

If you have the time: 1 Peter 2:4–10

I don't tend to feel very close to God when I'm at church. That might sound heretical, but there it is. I suspect I'm not the only one. We are all different, so it's no surprise that God meets us in different places in different ways.

There are a few places where I do find it easy to feel God's presence, however. One of them is in the bath (I won't go into detail about my bath-bomb obsession here). The other place is in the woods.

I was recently reminded of an area of woodland in Dorset, on a slope above a holiday cottage we rented one winter. The cottage was a beautiful old farmhouse, with access to a small indoor pool. It was luxury, contrasting against the turmoil we felt as we struggled with Sam's epilepsy and disability. The cottage was quite isolated on a narrow farm lane, and within a few days of our arrival it began to snow. It snowed so heavily that we could no longer get our car out: we were officially snowed in. Despite the five-mile hike to get milk and bread, it was an amazing experience.

One day, with childcare duties officially apportioned and agreed with Rachel, I had an hour to myself to wander up to the woods behind the house. I was pretty sure God would be up there. I turned off the muddy, slushy road down a footpath, which twisted through the woods. It was clear that I was the only human to have taken this path since the snow. Each step was a satisfying crunch mingled with a tinge of guilt for sullying the postcard-perfect trail.

The rhythmic crunching stopped short as the path turned along a hedgerow. Through the branches I could make out a white field of snow, but I also noticed a magnificent holly weaving through the hedge. Its dark green leaves and bright red berries were only just visible under the pillows of white. It looked the way holly trees are supposed to look at Christmas, and I was reminded of the carol *The Holly and the Ivy*, particularly the line: 'of all the trees that are in the wood, the holly bears the crown'. Standing by that holly with its glossy greenness and extravagant berries, surrounded by the dead-looking twigs and sticks of the other trees, it certainly was wearing a crown. But the crown the hymn is talking about is not just one of celebration and life in a dark winter wood. It is the crown of thorns.

So, did I find God in that wintery wood? I think I did. He told me a bit about how our lives can be at their most beautiful during the depths of winter. That our lives are beautiful *because* of the depths of winter. That they can be enhanced by seeing the fruit of our lives amidst the bitter, frigid temperatures.

He taught me that I can choose to hunker down and hide away and hope that spring will one day come, or, like the holly, I can reach out my leaves and even bear fruit.

That even in the hardest times, I can wear a crown.

Where do you feel closest to God?

It may be at the bottom of the garden or at the high altar at church.

It may be in bed, the bath, or along a country lane not far from home.

Wherever it is, think about this place. What makes it special for you?

THE VIEW AS A SINGLE PARENT
Emma's story

Mike and I broke up five years ago. One day he suddenly announced that he didn't want to be with me anymore. We had been together for over eleven years and married for a year and a half. It was a massive shock.

I simply hadn't seen it coming. I felt incredibly stupid and guilty. Here was the man I loved, telling me that he had been unhappy for years and I hadn't even noticed.

What sort of rubbish wife was I?

Mike continued to live at our flat for another month, and while he was there, I did everything I could to persuade him to stay. I suggested counselling; told him that I would try to change; I even took into account the list of things that he did not like about me (turns out it was quite long). It was no good. He didn't want to even attempt to fix our marriage.

I went to see my priest, who helped me see that Mike was definitely going to leave. I leant heavily on my family (my parents and two sisters) and my faith. There was a lot of praying going on.

I tried to focus all my thinking on our five-year-old son. I resolved to put my own feelings to one side so that he would believe that his father and I were still friends. Mike also said that this was what he wanted – so at least we agreed on something. But I was also really scared. Mike had always paid for our expenses and I was terrified that I wouldn't be able to afford to buy food for us both. I was able to pay the rent, but that was not going to be much good if we were going to starve.

I had my first uncontrollable public display of tears the day after Mike left, but there would be plenty more. I went to the benefits office and when the receptionist asked for my name, I started sobbing because I realised it would soon stop being my name.

I signed on for benefits but decided to stay at my job. It meant that I would be financially worse off, but I already felt like such a failure and my work was something I felt I needed to maintain my pride and dignity.

Then guilt started to pile up. I felt I had let God down because I was going to get a divorce. For months, every time I went to church, I would cry my way through the service. I sat tear-soaked and dazed, looking at the aisle I had walked down on my wedding day.

On the positive side, my friends in the congregation really supported me. They held my hand during the service, prayed, listened and kept the tissues in supply. I had only come to faith a couple of years before and was so thankful that I had this extra support.

My faith also gave me a sense of perspective. Although it was one of the worst times of my life, it reminded me that this period of mourning for my marriage, my future, and the traditional family life that I had been hoping for, would come to an end. I put my trust in God and allowed myself to go through all the emotions – the grief, the anger, the hurt, the feeling of betrayal, and, at times, the relief that this had happened so early on in our marriage.

Life as a single parent has actually not been as hard as I expected. Our son has autism, and at the time of our breakup he was not sleeping through the night. After five years of getting up every night, I was completely exhausted. It affected everything. I felt like my limbs were weighed down and my thoughts were pushing their way through molasses. Without exaggeration, everything I did felt like a massive effort and took an unbelievable amount of concentration.

Astoundingly, three days after Mike left, our son suddenly started to sleep through the night. If that wasn't God helping me out, then I don't know what is! There is no way that I would have coped with the divorce on the two to three hours of sleep per night that I had previously been getting.

I realise now that towards the end of our relationship, Mike and I were living very separate lives as I tried to protect his rest on his day off. Today, our son spends much more time with his dad and they have a better relationship than ever. The respite care that I was previously so desperate for now comes when our son spends alternate weekends with his dad. It gives me a chance to catch up on things, or just rest. It hasn't happened the way I wanted, but I try to make the most of a bad situation.

These days, I find that the hardest part of being a single parent is the small, daily decisions. I miss having someone to debrief with and share in the funny moments. My sisters are always on the end of the phone, but it's not the same as looking over at someone and feeling that unity in doing life together. I also find it hard when I'm having a bad day. These are the times when I feel the most isolated, and ultimately I am alone and having to make my way, a lot of the time in my own strength.

Our divorce was five years ago now, and to be honest, I have a good life. Mike and I continue to have a positive relationship and we work together to raise our son. We both get on well with each other's families, and I'm thankful that on special occasions, such as my son's first Communion, we were all able to celebrate as a family.

Although some days and weeks are tough, I will continue to try to be the best mum I can be. I will do all that is in my power for my son, and let God sort out the rest.

Emma (not her real name)

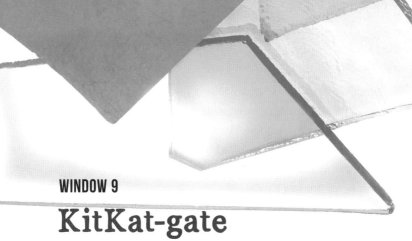

KitKat-gate
(Both of us)

'Jesus replied, "They do not need to go away. You give them something to eat."' (Matthew 14:16)

(Rachel's suggested verse)

If you have the time: Acts 15:36–41

There was an incident early on in our relationship now known as KitKat-gate. The re-telling varies depending on the narrator of the tale.

Rachel's version of the story:

Tim and I were in his room, in halls, during our first year of university (we went to different universities in London). On this particularly fateful day, I was feeling stressed, tired and in need of some tender care from a thoughtful, sensitive boyfriend.

I also needed chocolate.

I'm not proud of my emotional relationship with food. It seems my brain is wired to believe that I can eat away my emotions through a large packet of salt and vinegar crisps and a pot of hummus – or chocolate.

On the day in question, Tim had little or no food. His staple supply of pasta and pesto was long gone, and there certainly weren't any emotionally soothing treats available… except, that is, for one last KitKat.

Tim doesn't really like chocolate. He's a take it or leave it kind of person. He would rather have a starter than a pudding (whereas I think the sole reason for going out for a meal is the dessert).

Two important things then happened.

1. I expressed my ~~desire~~ need to eat the last KitKat.

2. Tim said he wasn't that fussed.

Then – and you might need to sit down for this – Tim proceeded to eat the whole KitKat.

All of it.

Every last bit.

Yes, the KitKat that has a natural split down the middle so it can be easily shared between two people.

Yes, even though he doesn't really like chocolate and wasn't fussed about eating it.

Yes, even though I had said I really wanted to eat it.

And… he did it with a little smirk on his face. (Tim has a particular, discreet expression that no one else notices but me. It comes out when he thinks he's about to do something very funny – but isn't.)

With such brazen disregard for me and my emotions, I did what every other self-respecting girlfriend would do in that situation: I began crying, grabbed my coat and left the room with Tim sitting bewildered, holding the redundant foil and red and white paper of a two-finger KitKat.

I then took one bus, one tube, and walked back to my own halls where I quietly and righteously seethed.

'The righteous eat to their hearts' content, but the stomach of the wicked goes hungry.' (Proverbs 13:25)
(Tim's suggested verse)

Tim's version of the story:
I had a KitKat.

It was my KitKat.

I ate the KitKat.

Rachel overreacted and stormed out.

There are many lessons we could pull out from this event. Maybe about how we care for those we love, and the benefits of open communication. Maybe something about the sacred nature of chocolate. The most important one, perhaps, is that we each look at situations from our own perspective.

It can be a shock to find that someone has earnestly held opinions that are completely opposed to our own. What starts as a different point of view can soon grow into disagreement, then conflict, then hurt and resentment; possibly even leading to relationship breakdown. Paul and Barnabas were mighty men of God whose disagreement meant they parted company (Acts 15:36–41). Finding a way to respect other points of view; seeing things from a different perspective; accepting that people can have opposing views to you and still be right; all of these things lead to reconciliation.

And then there is God's perspective.

His view is bigger, clearer, more tender, and full of love.

Move some hanging pictures, photos or ornaments to a different spot in your home this week.

See them afresh from a different angle and know that with all that is happening in your life, God has a different perspective.

Dare to pray and ask God to reveal some of His perspective.

Dare to pray and ask God to help you see the differing perspectives of others.

Comparison

(Rachel)

'Each one should test their own actions. Then they can take pride in themselves alone, without comparing themselves to someone else' (Galatians 6:4)

If you have the time: Psalm 73:1–6,25–28

I'm writing this in the springtime, and the clocks have just gone forward. Frankly I think I deserve a Nobel Prize for successfully changing the time on my car dashboard (though I suspect the oven will remain incorrect until autumn – I know my limitations).

As I reflect on this time of year, I realise the clocks going forward is a perfect lesson in the trappings of expectations and comparisons. My Facebook timeline would suggest that everyone (except those who worked a night shift) is feeling that they have lost out. Everyone seems utterly bereft at having lost a whole hour of precious sleep. We are all nurturing a sense of loss based on external factors. If I have to be somewhere at 7am on the day the clocks go back, and the alarm chirps into life at what feels like 5am instead of 6am, then that one less hour of sleep will feel painful, but I could have gone to bed an hour earlier. Sometimes I'm in bed at 10pm on a Saturday night – sometimes it's 11pm. Occasionally I dare to breach midnight, but rarely (and just saying that makes me feel old!). I know I will get less sleep when I go to bed later as none of my children have 'lie-in' in their vocabulary. But when it comes to the clocks changing, in real terms, nothing is actually different. My children, at least, will sleep as long as they normally would. The only difference is that external markers have changed. The clocks are telling me a different time, so I am persuaded to alter my expectations.

As the parent of a child with complex needs, much of what I find difficult in dealing with the challenges of life is tied up in how I see everyone else. Such disparity between my life and others' supercharges the teenager in me, screaming, 'It's not fair!' If left in my own little bubble, with no apparent 'standard' to set myself against, things might be quite different. If, as a first-time mum, I only had Sam as a marker, I could have easily celebrated his smile, joy and thick, squidgy wrists. But when I looked at my friends' children, my heart sank. They were grasping and looking, then sitting and rolling. Against their backdrop of galloping through milestones, Sam was missing out. With these comparisons, I felt a piercing sense of disappointment. Circumstances can be tough, but when you throw in comparison, it's like gasoline on the flame.

Theodore Roosevelt is purported to have said, 'Comparison is the thief of joy.' It's interesting how infrequently I compare my life to those worse off than me. There always are people who have it harder. I haven't travelled outside the 'first world' for over a decade and it is too easy for me to forget about the two-thirds of the world who live without basic, adequate food, sanitation, healthcare, education and equality – let alone all the other luxuries most of us enjoy.

Yes, the clocks have changed. Yes, what everyone else is doing makes a difference. Church will come around one hour earlier and I will need to rush to get there. I will juggle giving medications and milk at the right time, but my children will sleep as much as they were going to sleep, regardless of what the dials say on the wall.

There are an increasing number of books on Christian bookshelves about finding God in the difficult parts of life. It's as though it comes as a shock. Yet this difficult road isn't something that is talked about at length in Scripture. Why? Because a hard life was the norm. Women died in childbirth on a regular basis, men died in battle, starvation was real, and sickness was often life-threatening. People didn't need to be reminded that God could be found in testing times because that was the reality of how they sought God – *all the time*. What has changed is our expectation of how easy life ought to be, not the reality of life or how God works.

Living with the constraints of arbitrary external markers or grandiose expectations of what life will be like makes me feel more pressed, more resentful. Feeling squeezed by things I have no control over makes me believe I'm more restricted than I actually am.

While driving Sam to Great Ormond Street Hospital, we used to pass a brilliant mural on a wall. It said:

'Sorry, the lifestyle you have ordered is currently out of stock.'

When life is not what I ordered, I must live the life I have, not the one I expected. When I finally embrace my own version of today without comparing it to a false perception of someone else's social media feed or the dream I anticipated; when I learn to walk my life with the unique constraints, joys and beauty that only I experience; then I can step into true freedom.

Spot the difference.

Notice how, while making comparisons, we may have neglected to see that both pictures contain a beautiful landscape. Let go of comparisons and look up to appreciate your current view.

The great outdoors
(Tim)

'But ask the animals, and they will teach you,
or the birds in the sky, and they will tell you;
or speak to the earth, and it will teach you,
or let the fish in the sea inform you.' (Job 12:7–8)

If you have the time: Job 38:31–41

I feel most at home when I am standing in the woods, with
my trousers rolled up and my bare feet sinking into the cool
loam. Stepping between trees; observing the blooming fungi
and newly pecked holes in dead wood; all around, life teems.
So much is happening beyond our immediate attention and
it gives me great hope. I am comforted by the cycle of life and
death, decay and rebirth, all in the great outdoors.

The world around us has so much to teach. This is
particularly true if we choose to see ourselves as part of it
all. It seems to me that one of humankind's great arrogances
(and there are many) is to view ourselves as being somehow
above or apart from nature. It can be easy to mistake the real

world as being the cosy homes we create for ourselves, gently stewing in the fossil-fuel-powered, climate-controlled pods we live in. We have chilled cow-juice on tap, to add to our tea from China. We sip concentrated orange juice flown from Florida as we tuck into the plastic-packed pig's behind, which we put on our plate beside the mass-farmed chicken eggs... and that's just breakfast.

It's easy to joke about it, but all this seems so 'real' to us that a trip to the great outdoors is often a rare excursion; catching a glimpse of the stars a surprising pleasure. If we see all the wrappings and trappings of modern life as barriers between us and what is actually the real world, then that world might teach us a thing or two. Things our ancestors knew full well but we have long since pushed out and replaced with air-con, double glazing and microwavable slippers.

Wildlife can teach us about seasons and rhythm. We can experience a different perspective through the shadows and haze of day and night. We can begin to notice all the incredible things that happen right under our noses, but which we fail to observe. We can learn about balance and the careful equilibrium of life crafted through cold and warm, light and dark, life and death.

Step outside. There is no rush. When you are able, take some fresh air into your lungs. Touch nature around you – the warm sun on your skin, the damp earth, the cold wind bristling your hair.

Cherish where you are.

Literally step out beyond your borders, and while you are soaking up all you can sense around you, remember that you are part of a bigger world. Your story is part of a much bigger tale. When life is tricky it is easy to keep our heads down and plough on through, living in a bubble that only extends a few centimetres from our noses. Go outside, look up, and break out of that bubble.

TREE-HUGGER MEDITATION

Take this meditation outside, find a tree somewhere quiet and sit down (or use your imagination).

Stand under the tree's branches.

What can you smell? Could you smell what season you are in – the leafy damp scent of autumn, or the fresh aroma of spring?

Reach out and touch the trunk. Feel the rough and smooth of the bark; the fissures and breaks. Feel solid, immovable life beneath your fingers.

Now, feel time slow as you consider the pace this tree lives at. Consider its patience, slowly reaching to the sun. Think of its roots, running deep and wide under your feet, soaking up sustenance from the earth; rain, dirt, and decay; drawing up life.

See the leaves overhead, restoring the air we breathe, providing food, shelter and warmth.

Recognise how entwined you are with these slow, gentle giants. You are part of this bigger picture. Your story is part of this cycle of give and take, of growth and decay, of flourishing beauty.

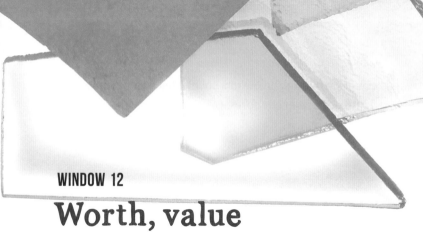

Worth, value and purpose

(Rachel)

'What is more, I consider everything a loss because of the surpassing worth of knowing Christ Jesus my Lord, for whose sake I have lost all things. I consider them garbage, that I may gain Christ and be found in him' (Philippians 3:8–9)

If you have the time: Philippians 3:4–14

'What's it worth?'

If you've ever been subjected to daytime television, you will have come across a variety of programmes based entirely on finding out what something is worth. Antiques, homes, treasures and junk are scrutinised, sometimes upcycled, evaluated and sold off to the highest bidder.

We do the same to people – assigning worth according to the size of our pay cheque, the newness of our car, the well-behaved-shiny-happiness of our children.

We try to weigh our own worth by these kinds of standards too:

Do I have a 'real' job or am I 'just' a housewife?
How can I be of value while being supported by benefits?
Being tired and busy will prove I'm important.
I've finally made it now I have a BMW...

We are constantly measuring ourselves and others – whether intentionally or not.

Sam's life challenges me that our measurements are askew. Sam is not financially, ecologically or physiologically valuable. His limbs don't work. He will never earn money, and the amount of waste product from his concoction of medical supplies is phenomenal. The financial burden he puts on health and social services far outweighs what I can ever pay back in taxes.

In this passage from Philippians 3, Paul is unpacking all the things he used to think were important. Here he is talking about his Jewish heritage. In other passages, he mentions his skills as a tentmaker (Acts 18:1–4) and not solely relying on the financial support of churches. In the middle of what reads as a little rant, Paul drops a clanger. He uses the word *skubala* to describe the value of his former life compared to knowing Christ. This word has been sanitised for our delicate post-Victorian ears, but *skubala* is a Greek word most closely translated as 's**t'. It means human or animal excrement. Paul is saying that everything else is a steaming pile of dung compared to what he has now in knowing Jesus.

I am so often lured into believing so many different things are important when actually they are simply... rubbish. Sam constantly re-aligns my vision of life as he puts things into perspective. It is tempting to gauge my life by what I do, what

I am capable of, how productive I am. But our value comes from being lovingly and purposefully created:

> '*So God created mankind in his own image,*
> *in the image of God he created them;*
> *male and female he created them.*'

(Genesis 1:27)

It is the purpose and creativity behind our making that gives us value, not our resultant productivity.

I am God's, and I bear His image.

Sam is God's, and he bears His image.

We are both wonderfully made (Psalm 139:14), and my love and compassion for Sam are based on a fundamental belief in his worth and value, not pity. Pity comes from the perspective of regretting another person's suffering or misfortune from a distance. Pity is sitting high and dry on a hill, looking down at the poor people in the muddy valley and feeling 'sorry' for them.

I try to practise 'value-based compassion'. Compassion is about doing away with hills and valleys and recognising we are all cherished – muddy feet and all. Value-based compassion is rooted in knowing we are all created in the image of God. The fact is, with all his limitations, Sam will have a much easier time entering heaven than you or I. He doesn't live with our layers of sin, pride, arrogance and hard-heartedness. Sam might have insurmountable hurdles created by an ableist society here on earth, but in heaven it will be smooth sailing.

I have wondered what heaven will be like. Will Sam not be disabled, or will heaven be so inclusive and accessible that his disabilities fade into insignificance? Will I be the one who, at the gates of heaven, feels disabled having to leave my arrogance, selfishness and pride behind while Sam wheels past me without a backward glance?

Our compassion for others and ourselves should pour from the same well. I believe others are worthy. I believe I am worthy. I am valuable because I am created. The same is true for you. Your worth is not tied up in what you do or have done, how much you earn or how 'successful' the world sees you as.

We are called to be heaven on earth, and in heaven we will all be celebrated for who we are in Christ because nothing else really matters. The one place each of us should feel valued and worthy is in a church community, not because of what we contribute but because of whose we are – God's, and what we are – a little bit of Jesus here on earth.

A very good friend of mine, Vanessa, once gave me a vase as a gift. If I tried to sell it, it would likely sit on the shelf of a second-hand shop for weeks. I doubt it would fetch anything at all at auction, but Vanessa spent a significant portion of her month's wages to buy it. Tim and I had worked with Vanessa in a clinic in Kampala, Uganda intermittently over several years. She had the best smile and a real passion for chicken and chips. When we last left Uganda (a year before Sam was born), she gave us the vase, with a precious and heartfelt message written inside.

A few years later, Vanessa tragically died during childbirth. To me, this pot is priceless because of the person, story and love it represents.

If I can treasure a misshapen pot, how much more valuable are we to the God who created us?

God sees you and loves you. He knows your value, your worth and your brilliance, and to Him you are priceless.

Find an object that means a lot to you but is worthless to anyone else.

You might describe it as having 'sentimental' value but actually it has real and tangible value. Its worth is not in its physical properties but is contained within its story.

Place it centre stage in your home.

Think and pray; what do you cherish in others? Text or call them and tell them.

What do you cherish in yourself?

THE VIEW AFTER YOUR DAUGHTER'S DEATH
Rachel and Dan's story

Rachel

Becoming a parent was flat out the worst day of my life.

My husband, Dan, and I had been married for four years when we found out we were expecting our first child. Scans came and went, and we watched our precious baby grow and develop. Around 30 weeks, I started to feel incredibly unwell. I spent a day or two lying on the sofa, sleeping and feeling rotten, with a bucket perched next to me.

That weekend, some friends of ours came to stay and despite feeling sick, I managed to do a few things. Then, I slowly realised the baby wasn't moving as before so I called the midwife, who advised us to go in – just to be on the safe side.

By the following morning, signs indicated that our baby was in distress and I was in labour. Immediately I was prepared for a Caesarean section. As an occupational therapist, I have worked with many premature children, so although we knew we faced a rocky road, I expected us all to go home in a couple of months.

On the morning of Sunday 6 March, Hannah Leslie Cole was born, beautiful and perfect.

Dan

When Hannah was born, I remember she did not make a sound. I went over to see her while the nurses were cleaning her up and could see her little chest rising up and down. She was so cute – just a little bundle. I remember looking down at her tiny hands and feet, touching her soft skin for the first time. Our baby girl. Our joy, however, quickly turned to concern as Hannah was whisked off to the Special Care Baby Unit (SCBU). Rachel and I were escorted back to the maternity ward, surrounded by healthy babies, while our daughter was along the corridor in SCBU.

We felt empty.

We had a long day of no news before I was allowed to spend some precious moments with Hannah. Little did I know that this would be the only daddy–daughter time we would experience. Suddenly, Hannah became unstable and, in the corridor by the special care baby unit, we were told there was nothing more they could do.

Rachel

In a room packed with medical equipment and monitors, Hannah was brought to us. She felt so light in our arms, but already grief and loss hung thick in the air. We took photographs, holding our flawless daughter as we tried to smile past our tear soaked eyes.

Hannah's beautiful button nose peaked out from under a knitted pink hat perched lightly on her head. How could something so fragile and small hold so much of our love and so many dreams? Wrapped in a white and peach crocheted blanket, we held Hannah in our arms as she breathed her last breath.

In that moment, our lives changed forever. We were parents but had no baby. We had to register our precious daughter's birth and, immediately afterwards, her death. We were thrown into having to arrange a funeral while clearing away baby equipment from our home. I felt like the bottom of my world had fallen from beneath me.

My milk coming in felt like a kick in the teeth. That night I was unable to sleep so I crept downstairs. Darkness surrounded me, and hours later Dan found me wailing from the deepest part of my being. The pain of a future of being a mother without a daughter was unbearable. I would never go wedding dress shopping with her, or hold her hand as she took her first steps. I was robbed of the only thing I'd ever wanted since I was young – to be someone's mummy.

Dan

The days that followed were dark and difficult. Looking back, I realise that I only started to bond with Hannah after she was born. Rachel had connected with her throughout the pregnancy, which meant we started our grief from different places.

As a driven, business-orientated kind of character, my mind never switches off. Working through my thoughts was a struggle. Where I would normally have turned to my faith and relationship with God, I found that my faith was not aiding the overdrive of my mind.

How could a God who loves me let this happen?

Did I really believe that God plans everything?

I had some serious questions and very few answers.

I decided to go for Christian counselling. With help, I realised that I was trying to justify God and defend Him, often coming up with even worse scenarios that could have happened. But, for my own sanity, the fact I had to accept was that sometimes, bad things happen – and I may never find out 'why' this side of heaven.

I felt I had no right to be angry with God. However, my pastor saw my conflicting emotions and suggested I try to let them out physically. After the obvious punch-bag was discounted, he suggested that I go out deep into the woods with a stick. It sounded out of character for me, but I took his advice. So one day, my pastor took me to a secluded place and I went off while he sat in the car (probably praying for me). I found a suitably large stick en route into the woods and began hitting and thrashing. It felt strange at first as it didn't come naturally, but as I spoke with God about my struggles and frustrations, I just swung the stick and beat the ground. Afterwards, I felt exhausted and remember collapsing back into my pastor's car. Surprisingly, this safe but very physical release of emotions was hugely helpful for me.

Rachel

The pain I felt during those first days can still hit me seven years later. The year Hannah would have started school, I felt like I had been hit by a bus as other people shared their 'first day' photos.

But despite the extreme pain, I also experienced exceptional peace. When we were discharged from hospital, we were flooded with cards, flowers and food. We felt surrounded by love. Our church family came every day for three weeks with hot meals. People cleaned our home, did food shopping, drove me places when I couldn't drive, and lavished God's love on us practically.

I've had counselling, I have been on anti-depressants and I've worked hard to not feel the need to justify my emotions. Some days are bad for no reason other than on that particular day it sucks that Hannah is not with us.

A while ago, I was listening to a sermon about the Japanese art of Kintsugi, where broken pots and plates are repaired with gold. Instead of hiding the brokenness, the gold highlights the cracks and makes the bowl stronger and more beautiful.

I want to learn to love the beauty that comes from my brokenness; to know there is beauty and strength which comes from having lost Hannah. In spite of everything, God remains faithful and the verses I cling to since Hannah's birth are from Isaiah 43:

> *'Do not fear, for I have redeemed you;*
> *I have summoned you by name; you are mine.*
> *When you pass through the waters,*
> *I will be with you;*
> *and when you pass through the rivers,*
> *they will not sweep over you.*
> *When you walk through the fire,*
> *you will not be burned;*
> *the flames will not set you ablaze.*
> *For I am the LORD your God'*

(Isaiah 43:1–3)

I know God is with me, and He was with me in my darkest days. He didn't let me be swept away in the rivers, nor burnt in the fire. Whatever life throws my way, I know God is good – and one day, I will see my baby girl again.

Rachel and Dan Cole

Why?
(Rachel)

'My God, my God, why have you forsaken me?
Why are you so far from saving me,
so far from my cries of anguish?' (Psalm 22:1)

If you have the time: Psalm 22:12–21

After Sam was born, we went on to have two more children. At the time of writing, Sam is 13, Jonah is 11 and Ethan is 3.

Toddlers can ask 'why?' several times a day.

'Why is blue, blue?'

'Why is it not snowing on Christmas Day?'

'Why is your tummy wobbly?'

They are inquisitive and enquiring. There are times when my 11-year-old also asks why, only it slips into an accusatory 'why?'.

'Why can't I play on the Xbox?'

'Why do I have to do my homework?'

When life gets tricky, when things fall apart, our whys can turn sour, quickly progressing from the toddler wanting more information to the teenager challenging with indignation and incredulity.

When Job's life fell apart, God finally responded to his question of 'why?' with a short-shrift response:

'Where were you when I laid the earth's foundation?
Tell me, if you understand.'

(Job 38:4)

God then went on to list a whole host of things that only the creator of the universe might know, rather than a mere mortal. So, it can be tempting to believe that such questioning of God is bad, wrong, sinful even.

'Why am I suffering?'

'Why did you let this happen?'

'Why do I feel so alone?'

Yet someone else in the Bible asked 'why?' of God – Jesus.

Hanging on a cross, Jesus mustered the strength through dry, cracked lips to echo words found in the Psalms:

'My God, my God, why have you abandoned me?'

(Matthew 27:46, *The Message*)

As Pete Greig in *God On Mute* points out, 'What an alarming question for God to ask God'.[3] It isn't easy to understand, but in one simple breath, our pleading for 'why' is validated by the Son of God. Our search for answers and understanding is given credence. In our darkest moment, when we are pleading for an explanation or throwing out incriminations, our 'why?' does not stand alone. Jesus has been there too.

I don't think I have ever asked why Sam was born with

a disability. As an A&E nurse, I saw tragedy breaking into people's lives, unexpected and uninvited, many times. I know how one moment can change a lifetime. But I did ask other whys.

Before Sam was born we thought God was calling us to live and work abroad, and had trained and travelled in preparation. We made plans expectant that this was where our lives were heading. After Sam's birth, we felt shackled to the UK, unable to live our previously held dreams. It was from this disappointment that I asked, 'Why? God, why give us a heart to serve and live abroad if all along this was going to happen? Why dangle dreams in front of our faces only to steal any chance of us living our hearts' desire – the hearts we believed You gave us?'

What happened next was much the same as for Jesus (and it's not often I can say that). No booming voice came from heaven. No deity spoke through a storm; nor did I hear a still, small voice giving me a thorough explanation. Having spoken with a thick tongue, caked in fear and uncertainty, I was left in the dark with my questions and confusion – 'Why have you abandoned me?'

That's OK. Sometimes the answers don't come easily but it remains important to ask.

What are you crying out?
  My God, my God, why...

Isolation
(Rachel)

'Jesus replied… "In this world you will have trouble."'
(John 16:31,33)

If you have the time: Psalm 139:1–12

As Tim and I stood with our feet under a hospital trolley, watching our son writhing and flinching through another potentially fatal seizure, my world felt small and isolated. It was as though I lived on an island, which at a distance looked similar to where everyone else lived, but on closer inspection had life-changing differences.

Sometimes, what made this sense of isolation worse were the words of loved ones intended as comfort. Although spoken with the best intentions, their platitudes were flimsy and weak, unable to take the weight of our heartache. Like the glare of the hospital lights when we stumbled in from the cold, dark streets, these words made us wince, deepening a sense of isolation and the desire to retreat.

The idea that God had singled me out to walk this road less

travelled also heightened my sense of loneliness. In my giant pity party, I could be persuaded that everyone else's problems were utterly trivial compared to mine. The impression that my little family were the only ones suffering stifled me. It wasn't until I abandoned the idea that suffering had been singled out for me that I found some freedom. Once I rejected the delusion that everyone else who follows Jesus is immune to the trauma and tragedies of life, I felt less alone in my fear and uncertainty, and my sense of isolation loosened.

The truth is, we are in really good company.

Ezekiel roamed the fields of dry bones of the land knowing that his own wife's corpse lay in the rubble of a fallen city (Ezekiel 37:1–3). Moses was a murderer; he didn't know who he was and spent his whole life chasing his own identity and hiding from his past (Exodus 2:12). Naomi's husband died; then her sons died and left her alone in a foreign land (Ruth 1:3–5). Paul spent his life focused in one direction, only to have a blinding light turn it upside down. Then, before he knew it, he had a thorn in his flesh, became a bit of jail bird, was stoned, beaten and shipwrecked – more than once (2 Corinthians 11:24–26).

We are not alone.

This isn't the first time suffering has happened.

These stories of our lives, of heartache and pain, are the same as they have always been. Thankfully though, God is within, around, beyond and inexplicably entwined in all we do and don't see.

Author Glennon Doyle has seen rock-bottom several times, and in her memoir she goes so far as to challenge us to lean into our pain, because it can become the energy for our purpose:

'You are not supposed to be happy all the time. Life hurts and it's hard. Not because you're doing it wrong, but because it hurts for everybody. Don't avoid the pain. You need it. It's meant for you. Be still with it, let it come, let it go, let it leave you with the fuel you'll burn to get your work done on this earth.'[4]

So, what can we learn from the lessons of the men and women who have gone before us?

God isn't an 'air-lift-out' kind of God. He isn't the 'make-it-all-better' King. God is a lying in a manger, hanging on a cross, walking in the dust next to us, longing us to shackle ourselves to Him so that we might share His yoke kind of deity.

We are not alone.

Ann Voskamp says that suffering shows us we are not in control, and the most crushing lie we are told is that life is supposed to avoid suffering, loss and brokenness.[5] I know that doesn't necessarily lessen our pain, but maybe it makes things a little easier to bear. We certainly don't need to worry about whether we have been singled out, because not only is suffering universal but a place of transformation. When we let go of believing suffering is unique to us, our sense of isolation crumbles. We might all have different struggles, but even Jesus told us that in this world we would have trouble. When we stop to consider that pain is not punishment, nor pleasure reward, we can stop grappling, open our hands and hearts and be present in our life – all of it.

History shows us we are not in control; that brokenness is universal. History also shows that God can be found everywhere; even on the tiny little islands we have built for ourselves.

Watch the news.

Choose a story that highlights others' suffering, and raise them up in prayer this evening. Pray that, like you, they will recognise that they are not alone in their distress.

> *'If I go up to the heavens, you are there;*
> *if I make my bed in the depths, you are there.'*
>
> **(Psalm 139:8)**

Emotions

(Rachel)

'Search me, God, and know my heart;
test me and know my anxious thoughts.' (Psalm 139:23)

If you have the time: 1 Samuel 1:9–20

Anyone who has watched the great Pixar animation *Inside Out* will know that all emotions are important. Sometimes I feel like I have been dragged through a hedge backwards by my emotions. I can go from lioness (fighting for my children's futures) to wet rag (crying in front of *Topsy and Tim*) in less than 60 seconds. As a parent of a child with disabilities, I often write emails and make phone calls that land on deaf ears. Part of life is fighting for services and navigating an endless number of appointments and therapies. I speak to over fifty professionals every year just about Sam; from his hoist engineer, to milk delivery man, to one of his four specialist consultants.

I can be articulate and professional when needed, but alone I might just as easily dissolve into a heap on the floor, utterly overwhelmed. I can be broken and tearful. I can feel steeped in heartache at Sam's inability to communicate effectively or express his daily pain. In the quiet, I am left with a bundle of emotions, struggling to contain each of them in my oh-so-small hands.

To make matters worse, I feel the pressure of a Christian myth that is sold to us from Sunday school onwards:

> *'If God is with you in something, then it will feel warm, fuzzy and lovely.'*

I'm told 'good' means 'nice'. That 'blessed' means 'easy'. Well-meaning people from church often say things like, 'It must make your situation so much easier knowing that you have Jesus with you.' This leaves me feeling that if life is hard, then I must be doing something really wrong. I'm duped into believing that 'hard' means 'bad'.

I can fall into the trap of trying to live an outwardly perfect version of my life. For me, motherhood has driven me towards an unhelpful form of false piety. It may be that relentlessly giving and always putting myself at the bottom of the pile feels like the gold standard of parenthood. Perhaps it's the delusion of a godly woman being quiet and quaint that's fuelling the fire. Yet, whoever we are and whatever we do, it is possible to fall foul of believing that possessing only positive emotions, and squashing all others, is the cornerstone of being a good person and faithful believer.

I've heard it said that, despite us having over thirty emotions, many people can only describe three – sad, happy and angry. Understanding the complexity of our emotions, and knowing we can feel several opposing emotions at any time, increases our emotional literacy. Understanding *how* we feel helps us work out *why* we feel a certain way and is a positive step towards living well.

On the other hand, holding my emotions too tight saps my energy. If I ignore the weight of them, they surreptitiously burden me more. Instead, I'm finding it is possible to learn to ride the waves; to experience all of my emotions, surfing the peaks and troughs that sweep through life on a daily basis. No emotion is bad. No emotion should be ignored. But, like an inflated balloon, it's the emotions we try to press that are most likely to blow. Instead, if we hold them gently, with time our emotions are most likely to slowly deflate all by themselves.

If I want the incredible highs of life, I have to endure the challenges and lows. If I want to reach the mountaintop, I have to keep moving, one step at a time, plodding up the ascent. The tearstained, snot-filled days give way to the smiling and precious moments.

Each have their own time. Each have their day.

Emotions aren't easy, nor vulnerability fun. Yet these seemingly conflicting emotions actually come hand in hand, wandering through my life like long-lost friends. The only reason I feel such deep emotions of heartache and grief is *because* of the depth and breadth of the unending and powerful love I have for my boys.

> *'It's important that when you're hurt you grieve. Otherwise you're anchoring your soul to a hurt that remains raw and will continue to hurt. Give yourself the time to feel what you're feeling without judgement or analysis.'*[6]

Drink tea, have a beer, look out of a window,
underline, colour and doodle around these words.
  Tell God how you feel – He won't be surprised,
and He really wants you to tell Him.

Learning to lament

(Tim)

'How long, LORD? Will you forget me for ever?
How long will you hide your face from me?' (Psalm 13:1)

If you have the time: Psalm 13

We have a habit of sanitising language. Not only is it very British to understate everything but it is also very Christian to avoid expletives and tie our tongues, especially in the midst of tragedy.

In the next couple of months, Sam will be having two major operations on his hips. It will be a time of long stays in hospital. We will be split between our children at home and Sam in hospital over an hour away. If all goes to plan, Sam will be in hospital for seven to ten days for each operation, one week apart. He will endure both of his legs being broken and then pinned in place, and possibly a bone graft. He won't be able to lie on his side like he has for the last decade; instead he will be placed in traction and suffer pain he is unable to fully express. We know it is coming, yet we can't explain it to him.

'Oh, bother, that's less than ideal' simply doesn't cut it.

When our friends ask me how I feel about this, it's much more likely I will give an honest and heartfelt stream of swearwords.

I am not a Greek or Hebrew expert, but my understanding is that there are several places in Scripture where we have sanitised the language to make it more palatable and respectable. Paul's swearing in Philippians 3:8 has to be watered down because we are taught in Sunday school not to use naughty words (see Window 12). Although it is good to acknowledge that language can cause offence, perhaps we have also hindered our ability to honestly express ourselves in prayer. Do you think God will be shocked or offended if you use a few four-letter words to honestly express your heart to Him?

The act of prayer is daring to speak with God, expecting that He wants to listen and supernaturally affect our lives. Prayer can take many forms, and in times of trouble a tearful lament may trip our lips (perhaps embellished with a few obscenities and expletives). Sometimes we just need to lay it all bare before God and ask Him to break into our sorrow.

It is good to lament, to cry out to God in anguish, but too often we want to skip the hard emotions and focus on the brighter ones. Sometimes we are even fooled into thinking this is what God wants us to do too. But instead of our Sunday best, God longs for us to come before Him dressed in the full robes of authenticity and honesty.

In their book *Option B*, Sheryl Sandberg and Adam Grant explore the healing power of writing after a traumatic event. Sheryl's husband died suddenly while on holiday, and she was left as a single parent to her two young daughters. As part of her journey, she wrote daily with truth and honesty. Turning her feelings into words was a means of processing what was going on. She found it brought clarity, and with time she could look back and see how far she had come.

There isn't anything you can say that God hasn't already heard. He isn't going to be offended, because He already knows. The foundation of any good relationship is being honest and open. So go on, put it out there. Lay it bare in front of God. Tell it how it is.

Write your own lament.

Take some encouragement from a master: reflect on this lament of David's and write or speak your own version, which reflects your own situation.

Be honest, be open and be real.

Scream and shout if you have to. Say whatever you need to say – your Sunday school teacher won't be listening, but God will.

'Long enough, GOD—
you've ignored me long enough.
I've looked at the back of your head
long enough. Long enough
I've carried this ton of trouble,
lived with a stomach full of pain.
Long enough my arrogant enemies
have looked down their noses at me.
Take a good look at me, GOD, my GOD;
I want to look life in the eye,
So no enemy can get the best of me

or laugh when I fall on my face.
I've thrown myself headlong into your arms—
I'm celebrating your rescue.
I'm singing at the top of my lungs,
I'm so full of answered prayers.'

(Psalm 13, *The Message*)

Your personal lament:

_____

_____

_____

_____

_____

_____

_____

_____

_____

_____

_____

_____

_____

_____

THE VIEW FROM WITHIN A FRAGILE RELATIONSHIP
Alex's story

My mum has suffered with a chronic mental health condition and insomnia since I was three years old. She is also an alcoholic. While there were 'normal' family times, I have memories of her spending all day in bed for weeks on end, and drinking every evening. Memories of when she was taken away in an ambulance following an overdose; of when she wrote to me via her solicitor to say I was no longer her daughter; or later in my twenties when I was with her through harrowing electroconvulsive therapy appointments.

My dad was a rock – and I am eternally grateful for everything he did in hugely difficult circumstances – but as I hit adulthood I felt ill-equipped for certain aspects of life due to a lack of maternal love, care, warmth and guidance.

I believe that our strengths and weaknesses can be closely aligned. My hungry heart and yearning for love led me into some unhelpful situations and relationships as a young woman, and it's a part of my life where I still battle shame. However, it also led me to God, community, friendship, marriage and children, and a career with purpose and great responsibility.

Through a wonderful place called Fellowship Afloat; through church communities where I lived; through my work in the criminal justice system; through a family of my own and through life-affirming friendships; I found places to belong. People have cared for me, taught me, helped me heal and grow, told me off when needed, and always cheered me on.

Learning to forgive was foundational for me, but I only truly recognised this much later on. In hindsight, it sounds pious to say that my mum needed my forgiveness – she was ill, after all – but it was something that I thought I needed to do as I searched for the cause to my discomfort. So, I prayed those 'I forgive you' prayers a lot, while getting on with my life and having sporadic (or no) contact with her.

She wouldn't come to my wedding when I was 29, and I didn't see her until after my second child was born when I was 35. However, those years of walking that path of forgiveness enabled my heart to melt when she asked to see her grandchildren, and we've taken small steps towards each other ever since then (although, if I'm honest, it can be two steps forward and one step back). And when, a little while after that, someone hurt me unexpectedly and deeply, forgiveness was my first and foremost response – not because it was easy, but because I hung on to it for dear life as the key to moving forward.

Being realistic in my expectations has taken me a bit longer to grasp, but I'm getting there with my mum now, accepting that she can't change her situation, and she can't be the sort of mum that others have. I am genuinely happy that we even have a relationship and that she is part of our lives in the ways she can be.

I was recently lamenting my frustration that, aged 48, I could sometimes allow my confidence to be knocked by a colleague's words. In a conversation with my husband I was asked if it helped to realise that not only is this person quite damaged, but I am too. And do you know what? It absolutely does.

Because even though I'm a believer in showing vulnerability, in being truthful and transparent about who I am and what's really going on, it's so easy to forget to offer ourselves the same allowances we would others. I am both humbled and proud to say that I am a 'work in progress' and all the fragile relationships I have shape me. They continue to keep me focused on my priorities, what's in my control and more importantly, what isn't.

Alex Osler

Guilt and shame

(Rachel)

'Therefore, there is now no condemnation for those who are in Christ Jesus' (Romans 8:1)

If you have the time: Isaiah 61:1–7

I have always had a way with guilt. For me, it's as natural as breathing – so when I became a mother, I made it my super-power. My capacity to feel guilt for any number of reasons is phenomenal.

Being Sam's mum means I always have something I could do for him. I have a relentless stream of 'could', 'should' and 'ought to' rolling around my head, fighting for attention. The fact that I'm a people-pleaser amplifies this rampant clamouring of tasks in my mind.

A few years ago, however, I realised that the feelings I thought were guilt didn't stem from things I could be sorry for. They weren't things to be forgiven. They were perceived failures; layers and layers of stuff that I thought was required of me. And when life is hard and we are required to slow down, the noises of guilt and failure in our heads can be cranked up to full volume.

It was only when I started looking into this more that I realised my problem wasn't so much guilt but shame. Author Brené Brown is a shame expert (if I have a choice I would like to be a chocolate or holiday expert, please), and I found her way of distinguishing between guilt and shame really helpful. She says that guilt is an emotion you can do something about; it stems from a mistake and has the potential to lead to positive change. When we are guilty, we might say, 'I did something bad.' But when we are gripped with shame, we think, 'I *am* bad.' Brown relates shame to a belief that our faults make us unworthy of love and belonging.[7]

When life is hard and things are tough, I am most vulnerable to believing that I am fundamentally unworthy. Yet God has pursued me since before I was born, relentlessly chasing after me with love and hope. And that sounding trumpet of love can drown everything else out, if I let it. It is one of my faith's paradoxes that I am both broken and entirely whole.

Every year, I drag my wetsuit down from the loft, dust it off and squeeze myself into it. For a good couple of years, it has been just a bit too small for me (or I am too big for it – whatever). So, the 'squeezing' has resulted in a ruby-red face and copious amounts of sweat. (I have thought about using talcum powder to ease the process but I worry I might step out of the sea leaving a trail of wallpaper paste in my wake.) Although the thick, tight fabric keeps me warm when I dive into the cold sea, when it is too tight, breathing also becomes a challenge. This dramatically reduces the pleasure of swimming or kayaking. For too long I have felt that being more godly would be like trying to lever myself into a wetsuit two sizes too small. I thought I needed to be a different shape or size than just being myself. I guess I thought God was calling me to abandon parts of who I am for something more holy.

As I embrace who God created me to be, I'm trying to choose my words much more carefully. When I feel bad because I have done something wrong, I stop myself from saying I'm a 'bad mum', especially around my children. I'm leading a loving revolution by example. I want my children to know I am worthy, even with guilt – and so are they.

The more I have slipped into saying the right words, my heart and mind have been opened up to really believing it too. For a long time after having children I lost sight of myself, of who I was, beyond being what everyone else needed me to be. Now, slowly but surely, I am allowing myself to dream of what I want to do and who I want to be, inspired by the knowledge that I am created, I belong, I am worthy and I am forgiven.

I have been helped on this journey more recently by Jo Saxton's book, *The Dream of You*, in which she leans on a solid truth: 'In order to know who we are, we need to know whose we are.' God hasn't given me a wetsuit that is too small. His wetsuit fits perfectly – if anything, it is one I can grow into as I become more myself in Him. It gently covers my skin, passing over the lumps and bumps of life. I am God's, here and now, just as I am; not when I'm fitter, better, fixed or holy. God has a dream of me, not one in which I am less than who I am, nor more like someone else, but a dream where I am more of myself. God's vision of me allows me to become *more* of who I am, with no squeezing required. If you can, create space in the next few days. Dare to dream. Dream about who you are and who God longs you to be, while remembering that He isn't interested in making you like anyone else, but simply the best version of you.

STICK MEDITATION

Find a stick or a thin piece of wood.

Think of this stick as 'should-wood'.

Sit with your should-wood and think about all the *should*s and *should-not*s that cloud your mind and sometimes drown you out.

You might want to sit with your piece of wood and do some whittling while you pray. As the sharp blade peels away the bark, meditate on the layers of expectations and pressures on you.

Or hold your piece of wood and feel the rough bark, the swirling stresses that knot into rough callouses; the bumps of the bark that indicate burdens of *should*, *would* and *ought*.

In the quiet, line them up. Think of each role, each expectation and each pressure you place on yourself.

Are they all there?

Once all your *should*s are heaped onto that stick, break it. Snap it. It ends here.

Abandon your *should*s for *could*s.

Leave behind *ought*s and embrace possibilities.

Forgiveness

(Tim)

'Which is easier: to say, "Your sins are forgiven," or to say, "Get up and walk"?' (Luke 5:23)

If you have the time: Luke 5:17–26

Forgiveness is hard, and increasingly countercultural. We are bathed in daily messages encouraging us to blame, claim, and complain. We are encouraged to find fault in everyone from our politicians to our plumber; if mistakes are made, we should point the finger and make them pay. We try to do this while simultaneously denying the mistakes we make ourselves, and the faults we hide on a daily basis.

Does this duplicitous approach to blame help us find peace? Does blame, claim, and complain ease the pain?

Holding on to blame is a bit like doing battle with a snake: if you let the thing go, it might just stop biting you.

Jesus is big on forgiveness – not surprising really as it was His life's work. While teaching in a packed house one day, with the crowd scrambling to get near Him, a group of people broke open the roof so they could lower their paralysed friend down at Jesus' feet. I imagine they were hoping for physical healing, but we read instead that Jesus saw their faith and said, 'Friend, your sins are forgiven.' Jesus saw that man very differently from the crowd around him. He did not see his physical paralysis as the priority; He saw a man who needed to know he was forgiven. When pushed by the religious leaders to explain Himself, Jesus healed the man of his physical paralysis too. He did this physical miracle only to emphasise the authority He had to perform the first and greater miracle of forgiveness.

The Early Church was encouraged to embrace forgiveness as a way of living in love with those around them. The letters Paul wrote to them – now making up a large chunk of the New Testament – were full of pleas for the people to forgive each other:

'Bear with each other and forgive one another if any of you has a grievance against someone. Forgive as the Lord forgave you.'

(Colossians 3:13)

It seems that receiving forgiveness and forgiving others is central to a healthy relationship with God and healthy relationships with others. So why can it be so hard?

If you have been hurt – and some of us have been hurt terribly and directly by people – forgiveness may feel like letting them off the hook. It can feel like a betrayal of all the pain we've suffered. It can feel like giving up the fight against the injustice and letting the perpetrators get away scot-free. This view of forgiveness deeply offends our sense of justice and raises our hackles.

But this is not what forgiveness is about. Forgiveness does

not negate the fight for justice. Forgiveness goes hand in hand with this fight. I believe that while addressing injustice, forgiveness places us on higher ground. We rise above the injustice. It's not about saying, 'It's OK that the snake bit me' – but it is about letting go of the snake.

You may have read stories about murder victims' families who have been able to forgive their loved one's murderer. The life-changing pain of loss has not been removed, but in their forgiveness, they are triumphant. They have finally disempowered the perpetrator, while at the same time raising the perpetrator up and saying, 'You are human too.' The loss is still raw, but the sting of the injustice has been defeated by forgiveness. The penetrating rot has been cut out.

How can we forgive like this?

Jesus ties receiving forgiveness and forgiving others together, as if they are the two sides of the same coin:

'And forgive us our debts,
  as we also have forgiven our debtors.'

(Matthew 6:12)

You can't have one without the other. To approach forgiveness, difficult though it is, we need to start with ourselves and acknowledge that we are broken. To see that we need forgiveness more than any physical healing. We start by looking at the plank in our own eyes first (Matthew 7:1–6). We can then approach forgiving others with the compassion of someone who first accepted forgiveness.

When Sam was born, the tragedy of his brain damage demanded an explanation. There were many areas of his care where we found ourselves pointing the finger of blame. Rachel and I approached this differently. Rachel, as the self-proclaimed queen of guilt, quickly found fault in the decisions we made and the things we did leading up to Sam's birth. The finger of blame pointed firmly at us. She also requested Sam's medical notes to trawl through what happened and find faults in the professionals who cared for Sam before and after his birth.

I, on the other hand took a 's**t happens' view of the tragedy, refusing to accept any blame for my actions and also not pointing the finger at anyone else. Bad stuff happens, I rationalised, so I just needed to accept this and move on.

I don't think either of our approaches was great. Rachel struggled to find forgiveness, particularly for herself. I, on the other hand, was blinded to the injustice. We have slowly changed positions over time: I have taken more note of the mistakes we and the medics made, and accepted forgiveness for this. Rachel has found peace in acknowledging that, though this was a mixture of misfortune and fault, offering and accepting forgiveness brings healing.

However, we occasionally both still find ourselves awake in the dark hours of the night, fighting a cold sweat, with a tight chest over what we did and what they did; we fight the snake again. When morning comes with its new mercies, we see that forgiveness is a long journey rather than a one-off event – but one we are committed to travelling.

KEYS MEDITATION

Go and get your keys.

They are going to help you unlock something inside and open the door to forgiveness.

Sit comfortably, then close your eyes.

Hold the bunch of keys in your hand.

Lightly feel the jumble of textures, points and curves.

Focus on the sensations of cold metal and smooth plastic.

Hold them more tightly. Slowly squeeze them in your hand.

Squeeze tighter, as if you are really afraid of losing them.

As you hold on tight, feel the discomfort of the keys pressing into your hands.

The pricking sensation, the ache, your fingers white with tension.

Your whole mind now focused on this one source of pain.

Why do we hold on to hurt, when holding harder makes it hurt more?

Slowly release the tension, allow the blood to flow back into your fingers.

Gradually open your hand and let go; feel the pain start to settle.

Let the keys fall to the floor. Feel the relief as the weight is lifted.

As the last of the discomfort fades, reflect on areas of hurt in your life you need to let go of.

Expectations

(Tim)

'Then Jesus said to his disciples: "Therefore I tell you, do not worry about your life, what you will eat; or about your body, what you will wear. For life is more than food, and the body more than clothes."' (Luke 12:22–23)

If you have the time: Matthew 11:25–30

Sometimes we have ridiculously high expectations of ourselves. This can certainly be an issue for me.

I once went through a period of time when I found anxiety at work overwhelming. I was working 50–60 hours a week as a General Practitioner at a large teaching practice. I had been qualified for five years and became a partner, taking on more responsibilities. At home, we had recently been through several traumatic years with Sam's difficult-to-control epilepsy. We were also keen to welcome other people to live with us, making our house a busy place. I was trying to be the perfect, fun, active dad for my two children (this was before Ethan was born) and also a loving, helpful husband for Rachel.

At church, I was responsible for groups meeting at our home as well as leading worship. Not being satisfied with this list, I decided I should run another marathon, aiming to achieve a personal best at the London Marathon in 2012.

In hindsight, it's not surprising that cracks started to appear in my mental health, but at the time I was truly surprised to find that shortly after the marathon (having missed my personal best by three minutes – should have tried harder) I found myself sitting at work with my heart pounding and my mouth dry, unable to focus on simple tasks.

My resilience had drained away and any suggestion of a complaint or confrontation would send me into a spin of barely contained panic. I could put the symptoms together and make the logical diagnosis of anxiety, but it came as a shock. I was sure that I didn't get sick, and I was definitely sure that I didn't have 'mental health problems'. I thought that we just needed a holiday, but after a lovely week in the New Forest I found myself returning to a world of stress and panic at work.

Much of my anxiety stems from a fear of failure, just as it does for many people. The perfectionist in me is never satisfied with what I've done, fearful that people will notice that I am less than perfect. The more we expect ourselves to achieve, the higher the chance that we fail to meet these expectations. If failure is unwelcome or feared, then we feel stressed and anxious about trying again next time. We need to either set the bar of expectation a little lower, or embrace failure – preferably both. In short, we need to be kinder to ourselves.

One of Rachel's all-time favourite books is R.J. Palacio's novel, *Wonder*, which is about a boy with facial abnormalities. The overriding message of the story is 'choose kind'. As a doctor, a father and a husband, I can choose kindness with ease, but when it comes to my own shortcomings I am often too hard on myself.

These days, as I sit in my consultation room, I still get stressed or anxious about things from time to time – and a large part of my journey has been learning to accept this. To be kind to myself and say, 'It's OK.' As I meet patients with depression or anxiety I am much more empathetic than I used to be. I can meet them where they are. I often find myself helping them cut some slack and develop practices of self-care. I encourage them to see the unreasonable pressure and expectation they have built into their lives. Sometimes I need to point out that self-care isn't self-indulgent, but simply the necessary rhythm of a sustainable life. I encourage them to see it's not just OK to fail but it's vitally important to fail – to embrace our failures before moving on.

As Christians, I think we often heighten our perfectionism further by believing depression or anxiety should not be experienced by faithful disciples. We are supposed to have 'the joy of the Lord' and not worry, like the lilies of the field (Luke 12:27). Personally, I've found a few books useful, including *I'm not supposed to feel like this: a Christian approach to anxiety and depression* by psychiatrist Chris Williams. I am also comforted by all those in Scripture who failed repeatedly, yet God still used them (Moses, David, Peter and Jonah, to name but a few). In fact, He wants us to let Him into every part of life, even the places we feel low or have messed things up.

If we let Him, God will take the burden from our shoulders and let us breathe out a sigh of relief. He isn't demanding perfection, He's calling us into relationship.

Heavenly Father, free me from the internal expectations I place on myself, driven by a fear of what others think of me. Help me to be kinder to myself, cut myself some slack, and have confidence in who I am in You. Amen.

Practising gratitude
(Tim)

'Do not be anxious about anything, but in every situation, by prayer and petition, with thanksgiving, present your requests to God.' (Philippians 4:6)

If you have the time: Philippians 4:4–9

For the first few years of his life, Sam seemed determined to spend birthdays in hospital. Other kids might dream of a bouncy castle in the garden or a party at the local swimming pool, but not Sam. It became a running joke that he could force out a fever or epileptic seizure, just to put a spanner in the works of any birthday or holiday plans we might have made.

We have many photos of Sam in hospital, looking dopey in a post-seizure stupor with cards and balloons around his bed. How could we celebrate Sam's birthday under those conditions? How could we exercise gratitude for the things God had given us?

Sam's birthday celebrations have since been more successful, but they are still a battle. The actual day he was born was probably the most traumatic day of my life. Watching helplessly as my newborn son stubbornly remained limp and blue despite attempts to resuscitate him is not the kind of memory you book a clown to celebrate. But that is exactly what we do. Sam's birthdays are an example of our stubborn commitment to being grateful for our amazing son, even though our gratitude is tangled in a web of hurt and flashbacks.

We celebrate Sam for who he is, as well as mourn the loss of who he will never be. We mix the joys of friends visiting, going out for a meal or taking Sam ten-pin bowling with the heartbreak of remembering the day of his birth. Tears and laughter share the same space on our faces the whole day. Despite the snotty noses and fatigue, it feels right to celebrate Sam in this way. It feels true to live with the conflicting emotions that are so poignantly distilled on his birthday.

It would probably be easier, however, if we were not under pressure from society (and even the Church) to be happy. Alongside the bombardment of happy faces on Facebook, society's narrative is that we should always be happy – and failing that, it is best to pretend so others don't notice the cracks.

The Bible talks of joy being different to happiness. It appears to be a deeper, longer-lasting, knowing experience, not a fleeting emotion brought on by a cat video on YouTube. Scripture tells us that joy is a fruit of the Spirit, but the danger is that we can reduce it to a quick fix. We tell ourselves that we 'get' joy when we 'get' the Holy Spirit, which in turn can be dangerously misunderstood that Spirit-filled people are always happy. But this is simply not true. If joy is a fruit of the Spirit then it takes time to grow. It needs to be nurtured and protected. If we're going through a season of drought, or our fruit is attacked by pesky blackbirds, there might be very little joy to be found on our tree. We might have to start again with buds and blossom until slowly the joy develops back with the Spirit's help.

One of the ways we grow and protect our little 'joy' fruits is through practising gratitude, choosing to thank God even when so much disheartens us. There is a great deal of wisdom in the saying 'count your blessings'. We might not be able to control everything we think or feel, but we can determine what our minds dwell on. When it is pouring with rain, we can choose to stay inside and sulk about our washed-out plans, or we can go outside with a coat on and marvel at the life-giving necessity of the heavens opening.

Actively thanking God and thanking others is a clear path to appreciating the good in life. Each small offering of thanks can work as a buffer against the waves of grief and sorrow. Rachel and I know that one day we will be devastated we can no longer celebrate Sam's birthday with him – and so for today, we are truly grateful. But practising gratitude has a more profound power: with gratitude, we can also learn to appreciate the difficulties in life. Just as Rachel and I take a deep breath before planning Sam's birthday celebrations, we have learnt to recognise that life's greatest challenges are often what we treasure most. Time and heartache have shaped and changed us, and cultivated areas of growth and beauty. For us, gratitude was the first significant step towards celebrating the lives we live.

Write: Every day throughout the next week, with your loved ones or just with God, voice three things you are grateful for. Write them down. Does it make a difference to your perspective?

1			
2			
3			
4			
5			
6			
7			

THE VIEW FROM LOSS
Hannah's story

My mum was so thrilled to become a grandparent. She loved children. She'd devoted her life to raising my siblings and me, and working as a nursery teacher in an infant school. As with so many other moments in my life, my mum guided and supported me as I entered motherhood myself.

My daughter was just a few months old when we moved in 2010. My husband had finished his training to become a Baptist minister and was placed in his first church. Adapting to becoming a mother and minister's wife, giving up work to be a stay-at-home parent and moving to another part of the country was difficult for me and I had some really low moments. There would be times when I would put myself down and compare myself to other mothers who, in my eyes, all seemed to be coping so much better. My mum was always there, listening and encouraging me.

Although it took a while, I finally felt at home in our new community and loved being a parent. It wasn't easy being so far from our wider family but we talked on the phone often and would visit each other regularly. These visits always involved a lot of tea drinking, chatting, laughing and playing with our little girl.

In January 2013, my husband, daughter and both sets of parents gathered around my hospital bed, where I sat holding another addition to our family. There was great excitement as we passed around our new little bundle and everyone talked about who he looked like. As we celebrated the arrival of our beautiful baby boy, we were blissfully unaware of how different things would be just 12 weeks later, when we would be gathering once again – but this time for Mum's funeral.

Although Mum had already undergone a year's treatment for breast cancer, nothing prepared us for the rapid decline in her health. It was a Monday afternoon in March and I was sitting at home, feeding my newborn son while reading a story to my little girl. My husband passed me the phone. It was my dad, calling to deliver the devastating news. The cancer had spread to Mum's brain.

I remember him saying, 'The only treatment that they can now offer is palliative.' The consultant predicted that she only had months to live. There was a silence as I sat, mouth wide open, my baby in my arms. Then came the wailing and the sobbing as I choked over the words, 'I can't! I can't do it! I can't be a mum without my mum!'

Mum died on 3 April 2013. I had stepped out of the hospital room to soothe my restless baby and as I rocked him to sleep, she took her last breath. I now faced the daunting prospect of motherhood without my mother; one of my closest friends, my wisest advisor, most dedicated supporter and the person who loved me unconditionally, in a way that no one would ever love me again.

Losing my mum, as I cared for a young son while struggling to keep up with a bright and energetic three-year-old, is an experience that I cannot fully describe. I will never forget my husband waking me to feed the baby one morning, only for me to respond, 'I don't want to do it. I can't be a mummy today.'

A lot of that year is a blur. Although there were some good times, underlying any feeling of happiness was a physical pain;

a heaviness in my stomach that just wouldn't go away. There was a deep sadness that Mum wasn't there to share moments with me. Sometimes it was simply that she would never see my daughter wear a new pair of shoes. Other times it was the bigger moments, like the first day at nursery school. More than anything, I missed sitting and having a cup of tea with her. The void left behind by the simplest interaction created the most profound absence in my heart. Someone told me bereavement is like learning to walk with a limp, and I agree.

My grief delayed our trying for another baby. As much as we had always wanted to have three children, I was hesitant to bring another child into the world, knowing that my mum would never meet him/her. I was anxious about caring for a newborn again, and associated it with losing Mum. But I also knew I couldn't let Mum's death stop me from living.

When she finally made an appearance, the arrival of baby number three couldn't have gone more to plan. My husband and I had decided that if we had a girl, we would name her after my mum. It felt like such a gift, and the whole experience has brought such healing. I love telling everyone I meet that my daughter is named after someone so special.

Experiencing such a huge loss at such a significant time has caused me to rethink the way I live my life. Our culture celebrates being strong, independent and successful in all areas of life, but more and more I've come to realise that we were not built to live this way. Vulnerability and brokenness are inevitable. When we accept our own weaknesses, and allow others to draw alongside us, the result can be something truly beautiful.

There is a danger in trying to present ourselves as a perfect, finished article – we protect others from seeing our vulnerabilities and fail to love each other in the truest sense. We don't have to pretend that we can do life alone. God gave us the Church – a bunch of broken people who, together, are being transformed by 'the grace of the Lord Jesus Christ, and the love of God, and the fellowship of the Holy Spirit' (2 Corinthians 13:14). It's messy, it's unpredictable and it doesn't always follow the script but it's beautiful, and gradually I am learning to become better at asking for and accepting help.

I feel incredibly grateful. For 27 years of my life, I had a wonderful mum who loved me unconditionally. She gave me life in more ways than one. Some people never receive the kind of love or devotion I did from her. I've heard it said that grief is the echo of love; for me that certainly rings true.

Hannah Goodliff

Help
(Tim)

'love one another. As I have loved you, so you must love one another. By this everyone will know that you are my disciples, if you love one another.' (John 13:34–35)

If you have the time: Exodus 17:8–13

One of my passions is trees and all things woodland (have I mentioned that yet?). I often feel like I was born in the wrong age, as though I belong to the time millennia ago when Britain was covered coast to coast in one large primordial forest. I'm sure I wouldn't have lasted very long against the wolves and the bears, but I would have liked to have seen it at least. As a kind of a nod towards this rather unrealistic dream, I manage a few acres of woodland in Kent. There are no wolves, but there are plenty of trees.

Every winter, I set about felling some of the very tall Corsican pines. I do this to clear some space for the native trees to flourish, and also to use the wood for a variety of things such as carved toadstools, benches, or firewood.

A typical session spent there sees me in my chainsaw safety gear, happily felling three or four massive pines. Getting them down is easy, as gravity does most of the hard work. The trouble is I never seem to plan for the next bit: what to do with the couple of tons of tree now lying on the ground?

As I set about logging and stacking the giant trunks, gravity is suddenly my nemesis. The job grows as my energy and daylight dwindle. As I try to shift another giant log, which is plainly too big for me, I ask myself, 'Why did I set out to do this on my own?' Rachel would say at this point, perhaps slightly condescendingly, 'Help is not a four-letter word.'

Asking for help is something many of us find difficult for a variety of reasons. For me in the woods, it's mostly poor planning and the fact I enjoy time on my own. However, often the roots of our help-phobia go down much deeper.

We have a lot of help looking after Sam. We greatly appreciate the support we get and love those who come to our home and assist us in caring for him. They become part of the family – but we still hate needing help. We would love to be able to cope without carers coming round five nights a week ensuring Sam is not fitting, giving him medications and turning him regularly to keep him comfortable. We know though, through bitter experience, that without this help the sleep deprivation is paralysing. To cope, to function, to experience anything like normal family life, we are fully dependent on a team of about eight people. We find this dependence difficult to come to terms with.

There are a lot of reasons why we as a family struggle to accept help. It may be the intrusion of privacy, or concern that others may not be doing it 'right'. There can also be a deep feeling of failure, or the belief that we 'should be able to do this on our own'. A big one is pride. Accepting help may in some way offend our ego. It can be painfully humbling to be dependent on others. But these barriers to accepting help all crumble when we learn to let go of the myth of independence. None of us are or should ever be independent. God created us for community, and we are missing out on something if independence is our goal. Moses' supernatural (God-given) power influencing the battle at Rephidim was dependent upon him raising his staff. When his arms got tired, he sat down and let his friends support him (Exodus 17:12).

Despite my solo antics in the woods, I believe God wants me to sit down and let my friends help. I'm created to be interdependent, not independent. I know I find it easier to help others than accept help myself, so what does that say about how I judge those who need help?

It's important that we also overcome the barriers to seeking help when we need professional assistance. If you are feeling low, or sick, or suffering abuse, seek the help of professionals as well as your friends. Allow your local GP, counsellor, solicitor, police officer or MP to become part of your team.

Community has to be a two-way street. The walls of fear and pride, erected to protect our independence, are unhelpful and ungodly. If we let our guard down, allowing people to help with life's burdens, we open ourselves up to experiencing a depth of God's love only tasted through vulnerability and interdependence.

Think about your current 'to do' list.

Can you think of something you need help with?

Take action now to contact someone and ask for help.

Notice how this simple action builds your relationship with them and benefits you both.

Sabbath

(Rachel)

'[Jesus] said to them, "Come with me by yourselves to a quiet place and get some rest."' (Mark 6:31)

If you have the time: Luke 6:5–7

'How are you?'

'I'm pretty busy, how are you?'

'Tired… and busy.'

Busy has become a status symbol. The need to answer emails on the go. The pressure to be indispensable and constantly in demand. Whether it's a tantruming two-year-old or a frenzied boss, obligations mean we are wanted and therefore important. Shauna Niequist calls it 'the hustle' in her book *Present Over Perfect* – the pursuit of worth through activity and busyness. The opposite of this is a confidence in our value that exceeds our productivity (Window 12). It is a peace that comes from our identity being established in who we are, not what we do.

The undercurrent of our obsession with busyness is that

we begin to believe that self-care and self-compassion equate to self-indulgence. Resting, having fun and relaxing have become seemingly unholy, yet God commands us to stop:

> *'Remember the Sabbath day by keeping it holy. Six days you shall labour and do all your work, but the seventh day is a sabbath to the LORD your God. On it you shall not do any work'*

> **(Exodus 20:8–10)**

God tells us to take a day off each week, and says that the absence of work, the calming of our mind and the resting of our body is sacred, hallowed and divine. He says we need to stop working in order to truly honour Him. God longs for space in our hearts and minds to step in and nurture us, heal us, and restore us for the work ahead.

For a long time I lost sight of this commandment, especially in the early years of Sam's life. I sought to prove myself as a mother through tasks. I sought to appease my guilt through a relentless drive to do my best. The practical reality is that weekends are my most busy time. Without school, and the respite it brings, Tim and I juggle our expectations of fun and relaxing family time with 24-hour care. It is hard and relentless.

After several years of spending more energy than we could replenish, we both got to the end of our rope. We stepped back from church and work commitments, and prioritised rest. With the help of my parents we carved out a day in the week as our 'Sabbath', when we created space and spent time with each other. We put aside drawing up medications nine times a day, hoisting, dressing, physiotherapy and constantly caring. There have been seasons when I've only been able to take an evening or just a single moment to create Sabbath because I have been unable to 'stop'. But this has to be short-lived because I know it is unsustainable.

Jewish tradition ushers in *Shabbat* by the lighting of candles and a spoken blessing. For a while we congregated as church in our home, and we marked the beginning of each gathering by lighting a candle while a child in our midst reminded us that Jesus was present and the light of the world.

When our family gave up electric lights for Lent one year, I quickly began to relish the lighting of candles in the evening. It was a sign that things would now slow down, shifting our pace and expectations. But our commitment for Lent was short-lived. Each night, the glare of a smartphone lightens my darkened bedroom, sparking thoughts and delaying sleep. Emails ping to interrupt mealtimes and conversations, distracting us from being fully present. Today, an act of Sabbath requires a considerable crafting of time and space that heralds a change in momentum, bringing a holy and reverend shift.

If I'm honest, I battle not to default to 'busy'. Tim routinely raises his eyebrows as I answer one last email or scribble one more note. I need to work on not letting my eyes drift towards my phone but ensuring the person I am speaking with is the most important thing to me at that moment.

I have to be deliberate about self-care, seeing it as sacred and rest as holy. One day I dream of someone asking me how I am, and with confidence my response being, 'I'm well-rested, thanks.' The real cherry on the cake would be to do so without recoiling from fear at what they may think of me. The truth is I still struggle not to justify my need for downtime – let's just say I'm working on it.

Light a candle and turn out the lights (obviously it needs to be dark outside).

As you take in the calming glow, consider how this light is the antidote to the glaring screen of your phone or your TV.

Consider lighting a candle before resting this evening, or the night before a day off, to signify marking the next few hours as holy, as Sabbath.

Finding a tribe

(Rachel)

'*Rejoice with those who rejoice; mourn with those who mourn.*' (Romans 12:15)

If you have the time: Romans 12:9–18

I've already written about how I have felt very isolated at times (Window 14). I soon discovered there were people who 'got it' and some people who didn't. There are those who saw me suffering and were happy to sit in the dust with me. Then there were those who struggled with my anguish and uncertainty, feeling the need to try to make things better. Unwittingly they would minimise my pain, by trying to point out the 'blessing' or show me a valuable lesson I was being 'taught'.

Initially, Job's friends were spot on:

'*When Job's three friends, Eliphaz the Temanite, Bildad the Shuhite and Zophar the Naamathite, heard about all the troubles that had come upon him, they set out from their homes and met together by agreement to go and sympathise with him and comfort him. When they saw him from a distance, they could hardly recognise him; they began to weep aloud, and they tore their robes and sprinkled dust on their heads. Then they sat on the ground with him for seven days and seven nights. No one said a word to him, because they saw how great his suffering was.'*

(Job 2:11–13)

The greatest thing we can do for someone who is struggling is show up; show up, and probably shut up. When Paul instructed his readers about what love in action looks like (Romans 12), it included mourning with those who mourn. In the years after Sam's birth, I realised that, on the whole, the people who thought they understood actually didn't, and those who said they had no idea what I was going through were the ones who took the time to listen and learn.

In *Love Warrior*, Glennon Doyle describes it this way:

'People who are hurting don't need Avoiders, Protectors, or Fixers. What we need are patient, loving witnesses. People to sit quietly and hold space for us. People to stand in helpful vigil to our pain.'[8]

As the years have rolled by, I have found that those who knew how to hold space in my grief and pain were the ones who were willing to walk this path alongside me. With time, our journey has been a mutually supportive experience. More than ever I value this tribe of (mostly) women who support each other through life. Some of these women I share beans with every week; others I message on an almost daily basis.

The type of support I can offer may be limited. In another

life, I might have been the domestic goddess who could whisk up an apple pie and a nourishing lasagne at the drop of a hat for someone in need (probably wearing a long floaty skirt and saintly glow). I doubt it though. I was always going to be an 'I'll order you a takeaway pizza' or a 'Let me get a supermarket to deliver an online shop to you' kind of person. But that is my version of showing up, showing solidarity, recognising the struggle and wanting to ease the pain.

With the advent of the internet and social media, I also have an online supportive network: groups and forums of fellow parents around the world with whom I can rant or celebrate; who understand the road I am travelling because they too are trundling down a similar path.

Whatever your story is, there is power in having a few people to share life with. Those who know all the details, so you don't have to explain yourself every time; those who bring sound, honest, supportive and perhaps difficult words into your life when you need it.

I encourage you to find the people who you can sit in a room with and be real, especially if they are willing to eat beans on toast* or drink tea with you. Tim runs with friends and goes out for a beer. Whatever it is, find the person or people who don't understand but want to, or those who really do get it and are willing to walk this road with you. We're called to live in community. We weren't created to do this alone.

---

*Once a week, I attend 'beans club'. Beans club meets every Monday from 12–2pm. Ingredients include: four friends, our pre-school children, a different home each week, beans on toast, and talking, laughing or crying (whichever is needed).

Who is in your tribe?

_____

_____

_____

_____

_____

_____

Who could be in your supportive network that you
need to try to connect with?

_____

_____

_____

_____

_____

Lord, show us the people in our lives who we can
support, and help us to find those who, when we
are tired, can hold up our hands. Amen.

Filling up
(Rachel)

'While Jesus was having dinner at Levi's house, many tax collectors and sinners were eating with him and his disciples, for there were many who followed him.'
(Mark 2:15)

If you have the time: Mark 6:30–34

You may have heard the saying, 'You can't pour from an empty cup'. We need the right balance in life of things that drain us and things that fill us up. For some, work simply drains. For others, work fills the soul. It might be a quiet night in or a loud night out, but if life doesn't have enough 'filling stations', we will find ourselves ragged and running on empty.

Jesus loved eating with friends. The Bible talks about it as much as His quiet times. It's tempting to over-spiritualise Jesus as someone who wafted around blessing people and generally being holy. But He was also a man. He laughed; He cried; He went to the toilet. He was a brother, a carpenter and friend. He clearly liked a glass of wine while reclining at a table, and though the Scriptures never mention it, I suspect He liked to chill out with a piece of wood and chisel. Like His father, in heaven and on earth, He was a creator.

It is tempting to slot our time into spiritual or practical, ministry or business, fun or edifying. But it is important to remember that Jesus was as much the Son of God in the 30 years before His ministry started, as at the time He was kicking off a global revival that would last for millennia. Jesus was as much the Son of God when He was living, learning and crafting His trade, as at the moment He was raised from the dead. We are God's chosen and loved children when we are near to tears with laughter, doing the laundry or speaking from a pulpit. But each of our lives needs filling stations – places and spaces where we are 'filled' and renewed for the work of life.

What parts of your day, your week or year renew and refresh you?

It might be something that takes five minutes (a quiet meditation), an evening (going out with friends), or a day (walking in the countryside). Here are the things that renew us. You may notice some themes. We both like the outdoors, but just one of us starts to tremor when he hasn't spent time in a wood in the past three weeks...

Here is the challenge: if you aren't doing enough filling up, your serving and loving and giving won't be as effective. You will feel as if you are walking through life carrying lead. Think about what fills you up and how you can be sure you are doing enough of those things.

Here are our lists to help get you started:

TIM

Sleeping in a woodland

Running

Napping (for two hours!)

A bath with bubbles, candles and the Radio 4 comedy podcast

A night in

Camping in a woodland

Being alone

Foraging in a woodland

A beer with friends

Reading (boring) books about history or science, mushrooms or trees

A meal out with the wife

Rough and tumble with three very different sons

Chainsawing things in a woodland

RACHEL

Watching a film that makes me laugh and cry

A night out

Reading chick-lit, John Grisham or an inspiring faith book

Hummus and salt and vinegar crisps (ideally round a campfire on my own, in the woods, but anywhere will do)

Lunch with friends

Date night with Tim

Time alone

A nap (20 mins most days)

Finishing a run (not starting one)

Listening to music

Making memories with the children

What's on your list?

_____

_____

_____

_____

_____

_____

Do you spend enough time on these things? How could you increase the time you spend filling up?

_____

_____

_____

_____

_____

_____

THE VIEW AS A SURVIVOR OF ABUSE
John's story (written by Tim)

When you first meet John, it's not just his finely waxed, upturned moustache that leaves an impression – it's his wholeheartedness. He has a real gift for making people feel welcome. Whoever you are, whatever your struggle, John literally welcomes you with open arms.

John's attitude to life, however, was not born easy. He didn't become the gentle and compassionate man he is today by sitting in a pew listening to sermons, or going on a two-week mission trip to sub-Saharan Africa. His love for the broken, the afflicted, and the marginalised did not come from studying the Beatitudes or reading C.S. Lewis. Much of who John is today is both because of and in spite of the terrible experiences of his childhood.

John is a survivor of child abuse. He is a survivor of the years of turmoil that follow abuse. He is a survivor of alcohol and drug abuse. But above all that, John is John.

Between the ages of 8 and 14, John was the victim of sexual abuse by his father's employer, a close friend of the family. His abuser was someone who was a highly respected and trusted member of the community. According to his abuser, however, John was 'too nice a boy' and needed to become 'more worldly'.

Having formerly been a happy and settled lad, John's behaviour became increasingly erratic. He started skipping school and plummeted out of the top sets, and by the age of 14 took up an interest in alcohol. His attendance at school was so sporadic that his teachers didn't recognise him. His abuser had convinced him that no one would believe him if he disclosed what was really going on. Keeping it secret, John searched for some sort of relief from his pain, being heavily reliant on alcohol by his late teens.

Eventually, John found the strength to confide in his older brother, who encouraged him to tell their parents what had happened. Remembering this difficult conversation, John recalls with great sadness how the abuse also damaged his relationship with his father:

> 'It only takes a few seconds to not only destroy the trust you have in your father, but likewise the faith your father has in his own abilities as a parent. The moment my father asked if I was sure the abuse had really happened, we both knew our relationship was shattered. It is the last thing any victim of abuse wants to hear from a loved one. Unfortunately, my father died not long after and my greatest regret was that he didn't live long enough for us to fully repair our relationship.'

John tried seeking help from health professionals at this time, but having been told to 'pull his socks up' by a GP at the age of 16, John lost confidence that there was anyone out there willing to help. At the age of 18 he took an overdose and, under psychiatric services, was diagnosed with obsessive compulsive disorder as well as anxiety and depression. His psychiatrist suggested he should try to just 'forget' the abuse, but in an attempt to do just that, John turned deeper into drugs and alcohol.

By the age of 27, John was living a shadow of a life, both physically and mentally. He sought help from Survivors UK, a London-based charity, and entered into three years of therapy. As John slowly started to regain some love and respect for himself, he also reignited a spark of compassion for others. Shortly before the therapy finished, he enrolled himself on a therapist training course and, after qualifying, began voluntary work.

John left London with his partner, Yvonne, who supported him during his recovery, and they moved to Colchester. It was there he began volunteering for, and eventually managing, the organisation HEAL (Helping Everyone Abused Live). Under his leadership, the organisation became a registered charity and was awarded the Queen's Award for Voluntary Services in 2006. A lifelong love of the outdoors prompted John to undertake professional training in bushcraft and survival, and in 2007 John left HEAL to co-found the charity Greenpath Ventures. One of Greenpath Ventures' roles is to support disadvantaged individuals to gain self-reliance and confidence by learning bushcraft and survival skills.

However, John's determination was further tested when, shortly after his Arctic survival training in 2008, he was diagnosed with a broken back. Following a complex operation to fuse his lower spine, and lengthy rehabilitation, John felt ready to bounce back again. He undertook jungle survival training in the Amazon in 2012 and Sahara survival training in 2014, bringing back a wealth of skills to share.

In addition to teaching bushcraft skills to a wide range of people, John continues to support survivors of abuse through another charity he started called AARCA (Assisting Adult Recovery from Child Abuse). Both charities positively impact many struggling individuals with John's values of welcome and recovery. In his own words:

'I am very passionate that people can move from being victims of abuse to survivors of abuse. I also want people to know that they do not have to be defined by either their abuse or mental health diagnosis; that people are much more than this.'

John carries the scars of his traumatic life and it is these scars that make up some of who he is. His story is not one of 'and now it's all better'; he continues to live with ongoing mental health issues, not to mention the demands of family life, an overactive dog, and the stress of maintaining such a perfect moustache.

Healing does not mean forgetting the past as John's psychiatrist once told him. John's healing is an active, dynamic thing. It grows and changes and is ongoing. It bears fruit, draws no lines, erases no memories but creates new and greater things out of adversity.

John would not call himself a Christian, but he has Jesus' values at his very core. To me, his life is an example of God's messy, unfathomable, incarnational love for us. John has been through his own kind of death and resurrection and has turned his story into one of generous, extravagant compassion. He is, therefore, one of the godliest men I know.

John Wills (written by Tim)

Lessons in the dark

(Tim)

'The heavens declare the glory of God; the skies proclaim the work of his hands. Day after day they pour forth speech; night after night they reveal knowledge.'
(Psalm 19:1–2)

If you have the time: Genesis 1:1–5

I remember the time I first experienced true pitch darkness, seeing absolutely nothing around me. I was about 11 years old and on a day trip to Norwich with my grandad. These trips were much anticipated and tended to be a yearly event, usually sometime around my birthday. I'm one of six children, so looking back, our day trips must have kept Grandad quite busy throughout the year.

We had spent time wandering around Norwich, finding tacky sunglasses for me to buy in the market with Grandad talking about the local history, interspersed with his usual wartime stories. Then we went to the castle. While on a tour of the dungeons we descended into the damp belly of the place.

The guide explained that we were in a pit where prisoners were thrown and left to die, often on top of already decaying corpses (not a very tasteful image – but when you are 11, the gorier the history lesson, the better).

The guide then said he would turn the lights out 'just for a minute', allowing us to experience the darkness. I was not particularly scared at this idea – I'd seen 'darkness' before, every night in fact. But when the lights went off I instantly realised this was different. The stone walls, the group of 20 or so tourists, my grandad, the guide – all of it disappeared into inky blackness before my eyes. I was immediately floating on a pitch-black lake, with no bearings, tether or direction. I unconsciously reached out for Grandad's hand and we stood there, holding hands, for the long minute of darkness. I remember feeling a little embarrassed having grabbed his hand, but at the same time, scared enough not to let go.

Darkness is something we fear. It's something we avoid. It is something that stops us seeing everything around us clearly. It's something to banish. We see darkness as bad and light as good, and we carry this literal black-and-white thinking around with us through our dawns and dusks. We expel all dark from our houses, preferring artificial light from waking to sleeping rather than accepting that the earth spins and the sun might have moved on for another day.

Rachel's already said that our family gave up electric lighting for Lent one year. It was one of the few Lenten fasts that actually got easier as time went on because the evenings lengthened. We lit candles and used a few paraffin lamps. We accepted that we had to move more slowly around the house in the dark. We abandoned work at sunset, and we mostly managed without mishap.

Quickly, we learned to prepare for the darkness. We grew to love the shadows and flickering candlelight, while developing a strong dislike of the harsh brightness of electric lighting. Unable to turn off the fridge light, opening the door now sent a shock to our retinas, making Rachel's eyes squint and face distort as she hunted for a snack.

As time went on we realised we were sleeping better, and earlier. The darkness brought peace. The sun going down was noted and welcomed. It meant the day was done and it was OK to slow down, to accept that no more could be done until the sun returned with a new day. The darkness brought release from daylight-related activity. But despite us all agreeing that we did not like electric lighting anymore, after Lent passed we soon picked up our old habits, suddenly banishing sundown with the thoughtless flick of a switch.

Darkness is part of living – a part that does not necessarily need to be extinguished as quickly as possible. In her book *Learning to Walk in the Dark*, Barbara Brown Taylor talks about how the dark night of the soul doesn't need to be sprinted through as quickly as possible. She suggests this:

> 'When we run from darkness, how much do we really know about what we are running from? If we turn away from darkness on principle, doing everything we can to avoid it because there is simply no telling what it contains, isn't there a chance that what we are running from is God?'[9]

Maybe there is much to be appreciated and seen in the darkness. In fact, it is only in the darkness that we can wonder at the incomprehensible magnitude and unfathomable splendour of a starlit sky, expanding light years across a galaxy of which our planet is only a tiny speck.

We are created to live in both light and darkness; to exist in the passing rhythms of life. Our brains need darkness to trigger sleep and the rising sun to waken our slumber.

Day and night. Sunrise and sunset.

We can appreciate the warmth of the midday sun, and look forward to the quiet beauty of the night. Sometimes darkness can be scary, but that's OK too. When we can't see a way through, wherever we are, we can always reach out for God's hand. He might not switch on the light but He is always there. He is waiting, eager to hold our hand and wait in the darkness with us.

IN-THE-DARK MEDITATION

Turn off the light.

Get comfortable in the darkness. Sit in this monochrome world.

Darkness is not frantic. It can usher in calm.

Take time to let your eyes adjust. What shapes and shadows can you see?

How has the blanket of darkness changed everything around you? How has it changed you?

How do you feel – fearful or at peace? Agitated or sleepy?

Breathe in and out, and focus on your other senses.

Listen. Touch. Smell.

Welcome God in to the darkness.

Rest with Him and listen to what He has to say.

Abundant living

(Rachel)

'The thief comes only to steal and kill and destroy; I have come that they may have life, and have it to the full.'
(John 10:10)

If you have the time: 1 Kings 19:1–9

Many times Tim and I have stood shoulder to shoulder as medical staff buzzed around trying to stop one of Sam's potentially life-threatening seizures. These repeated experiences, along with our own medical expertise, mean we are well placed to assess the standard of care during traumatic events. Having discussed this, we firmly agree that a good standard by which to compare A&E resus departments is how long it takes for parents to be offered a cup of tea. When the world is falling apart, gripping a polystyrene cup of steaming hot beverage is, somehow, comforting.

This might seem flippant (and probably shows the kind of humour we adopt during such harrowing episodes) but it is also the paradox of life. In every situation and season there needs to be light and dark, humour and seriousness, hard work and tea breaks. We are physical, spiritual and emotional beings who have physical, emotional and spiritual needs.

At times when my life has been particularly stretched, when the weight of emotions and to-do lists have bowed my shoulders and buckled my knees, I have abandoned fun, relaxation and creativity for seemingly more important things. I have gone into survival mode. But with time I have realised that just about scraping through each day is unsustainable. A life lived solely from task to task, fighting off the immediate pressures and barely managing to cover the essentials, becomes hollow.

On a fundamental level, life becomes dramatically more difficult when we don't look after our physical needs. I have a tendency to get 'hangry' (the kind of anger fuelled by hunger). I also know that living on not enough sleep is like walking through treacle. Eating well and sleeping enough is easy to type (or read), but actually doing it sometimes requires significant effort and changes in my life choices. Before I can build anything of an abundant life, I need to begin with looking after my body. And it was the same for Elijah – on a turbulent journey, angels encouraged him to eat and sleep, to supplement his strength and prepare for the trials ahead (1 Kings 19:1–9).

John 10:10 is a verse we cling to, to insist on our right to a good life. Jesus says He came to give us life to the full.

But what constitutes living life to the full?

A full glass means 'drink filled right to the top' – right?

But is that the same for our lives?

Is abundance a jam-packed life?

A defining book for both Tim and me was *The Chimp*

Paradox by Steve Peters. It's a very readable but challenging psychology book that looks at how our brains work, what motivates us and what constitutes a 'happy and successful' life. One thing Peters says is that each of us have a 'stone of life' that represents our deepest held values and the things we see as important. He suggests that if the life we live does not reflect our 'stone of life', we will ultimately feel unsatisfied.[10] We will not feel we are living an abundant life.

If my top three priorities are my relationship with God, my relationship with my husband and my children, but then I spend all my time doing things at church and working every other day of the week, I will feel unhappy and unbalanced. For me, my relationship with God needs space and quiet. I need time listening to others of faith and worshipping – often alone. Equally, I need to sit across the table from my husband, look into his eyes and remember who I'm doing life with. It's good to be reminded that he's still my favourite person, and for us to enjoy being together.

But more than anything, I believe 'abundance' in life is about letting go – letting go of busyness, letting go of cramming every day and every minute, and instead valuing space, peace and fun.

God created me to be creative (and that is true for everyone), but so often I can treat creativity as if it isn't important. It doesn't feel as valuable without some tangible outcome or useful product at the end of the day. But when life is particularly hectic, I know I need that space even more.

Abundance is not dependent on more, but less.

Abundance needs margins: gaps of space between work at work and work at home; space between one Monday and the next Monday; space between emails and the washing and the leaking garage roof. It is about making time for naps, for writing, for listening and for reading. Most importantly I need time to watch a romantic comedy that my husband would roll his eyes at, without him being in the room tutting.

As a parent, I can be tricked into thinking being a good mum means putting my children first at the expense of my own needs. You get on a plane, however, and the safety instructions tell you to put on your own oxygen mask first *before* helping others – and with very good reason. Abundance comes from ensuring our needs are cared for too. We need to be fed, rested, and supported so that we can work, create, and have fun.

Creating the space and margins needed for abundance enables us to allow certainty and control to melt away. In their place comes the opportunity for belief in a mysterious, unfathomable creator God who is interested in every aspect of our lives.

We need room in our lives to allow for the opportunity of abundance. What can you stop doing, abandon or strike off the to-do list in order to create margins and give yourself space?

_____

_____

_____

_____

_____

Choosing easy

(Rachel)

'Jesus said to her, "I am the resurrection and the life.
The one who believes in me will live, even though they die"'
(John 11:25)

If you have the time: Luke 18:18–27

Let's play a game.

Look at the list below and delete from either the left or right column as appropriate.

Which would you prefer?

Fruit salad	Cream cake
Marion Keyes	Hilary Mantel
Dave channel	Discovery Channel
Walking along the beach	Hiking up a mountain
Walking in the sun	Walking in the rain
Gentle breeze	Howling gale
Pavement	Countryside track

Disabled son	Neuro-typical daughter
Lie-in	Morning run
Living in Essex	Living in Ethiopia
Refining fire	Anointing oil
Cross	Resurrection

I don't know about you, but I have a tendency to choose 'easy'. Tim is a Discovery Channel, morning run (after a lie-in) and Hilary Mantel kind of person. When I sit on the sofa, I want to relax, not be made to think about what I'm watching. When I pick up a book, I want to escape to a fictional world where the protagonist gets to kiss her dream man as the sun sets. I want to be inspired, without the need for too many long words. That means, if I'm totally honest, I would choose the non-disabled son over the disabled one. I want the easy road, not the hard one.

But I've discovered hard is not the same as bad.

This is most beautifully demonstrated when we camp down at the woodland. Whether I go on my own or with the family, every part of life is harder in the woods. With no running water, no hot tap, no flushing toilet, no gas cooker, no TV or comfy sofa, all the basic experiences of life are challenging. To make a cup of tea, Tim needs to have felled a tree the year before, hauled it across the ground and used a chainsaw to cut it. Then it is split and piled up to dry for a year. Once we have moved it to the wood store it then needs to be split again before building a fire, first into small strips of kindling and then larger logs. Using a fire steel and cotton wool, the spark catches light and slowly the flames gobble up the dry and combustible wood. Having carted several litres of water from home, I fill a kettle and place it over the fire on a grill supported by two large logs. When the tea is finally ready, it tastes so much better than any tea from an electric kettle ever could.

It seems that kingdom values marry quite well with woodland values. All that is important for followers of Jesus – love, perseverance, hope and faith – comes out of 'hard' times. They are all more potent, more real and more tangible with time and through trials. Of course I would like to come to the place of depending on God, relying on His voice and searching for hope when everything is going dandy, but it simply doesn't happen. Transformation, sacrifice and refining all seem to require the hard road, because that is where the hope and perseverance is tended and grown. It's the rough roads that bring the best view, not the easy one. Quite simply, if we want the power of the resurrection, we have to walk through the transformation of the cross.

What things in your life are difficult but their challenge increases their value?

(Going for a run, camping, BBQ, crochet, knitting, getting out of bed when the dark clouds of depression loom...)

_____

_____

_____

_____

_____

All of me

(Rachel)

'If we are thrown into the blazing furnace, the God we serve is able to deliver us from it, and he will deliver us from Your Majesty's hand. But even if he does not, we want you to know, Your Majesty, that we will not serve your gods or worship the image of gold you have set up.'
(Daniel 3:17–18)

If you have the time: Matthew 16:21–27

'Mum, can I go trick-or-treating?' asked a six-year-old Jonah.

'Well, we don't normally go trick-or-treating,' I replied.

'But I want to dress up as a ghost.'

'Yep, that's the kind of thing people dress up as…'

'I want to go with Sam and Dad. Then together we can go as the Father, Son and Holy Spirit.'

I posted this on Facebook and was flooded with comments, likes and laughing emojis. Jonah's perspective and humour are wonderful and, being honest, I'm delighted to share them as I think they show me in a good light. I pick and choose what I share with the outside world. I decide which parts to divulge. Whether it is the truth about my spiritual life, my children's misbehaviour or my impatience and struggles, there are bits I project and some I hide.

One Saturday, I sat in the balcony of a big church outside London. The speaker, Shauna Neiquist, was sharing her view of how our lives are made up of seasons. Her message was that we need to embrace the season we are in, and recognise that it too will pass. I sat and wept because I could not see a next season that wasn't 'winter': it would either be hard, grafting, running on empty, always giving more than I had to give; or my son would die, leaving me with a gaping hole of grief in my life.

I cried and inwardly resented those sitting next to me, who I assumed all had perfectly happy lives. I was becoming pious about how my situation was so much worse than everyone else's when the worship band began playing and led us in the song *Take All of Me*.[11] Just a couple of minutes later I heard myself singing the words, 'Jesus Christ, take my life, take all of me'.

I stopped in my tracks. I had sung that song dozens of times, yet it seemed I never really meant it. When I said 'all of me', I actually meant 'but let me control this bit'. Or even, 'don't take this from me, Lord, I like this bit'. When I sang, 'all of me', what I really meant was 'I'm giving you the bits I want to, as long as they all go to plan and work out fine'. I was negotiating a fine balancing act of give and take, unlike Shadrach, Meshach and Abednego who proclaimed their devotion to God regardless of the outcome (Daniel 3:18). A bit like choosing which version of life I show to others, I was limiting God's sovereignty to only some parts of my life. I wasn't being authentic with Him.

It isn't appropriate to share *everything* on social media, and it's important to recognise that others are sharing the edited and cropped version of their lives. It is healthy to share the real 'us' with a few people, while holding the 'Facebook version' of life very loosely, whether it is the one we expected or the one we think others expect from us.

God is calling me into a relationship with Him where I give every aspect of my life. Not just the good bits, the funny parts, the publicly acceptable bits, but *everything*. Sitting towards the back of the church, on the left, singing away, I was suddenly struck by how little I was actually prepared to surrender my life, or more importantly, how unwilling I was to let go of the image of what my life was 'supposed' to look like.

Look around your home and find something to give away. Find something that you will miss – something that means a lot to you, which a friend would really appreciate. It could be a souvenir from a holiday or an ornament you treasure. It could be your favourite screwdriver or the pen you use most.

Reflect on how it feels to give this thing up.

Reflect on how much more it means when giving away something close to your heart.

Ask God to show you the areas of your life you need to give over to Him.

THE VIEW AS THE MOTHER OF JESUS
Mary's story

I didn't know a man could snore* so loudly.

I guess there is comfort in its constant drone, though. With my husband asleep next to me, I feel less alone. And as I lie here breastfeeding this perfect bundle of love, I am filled with hope and endless questions.

Am I doing it right?

Is he latched on correctly?

Is he supposed to be sick like that?

What does his screwed-up face mean?

Did I feed him too much? Or not enough?

Is it supposed to hurt this much?

I wish my mum was here. She would know what to do – she always knows what to do. I guess I always thought she'd be next to me. I certainly imagined her with me when I had my first child. But none of this is how I imagined. I wonder what she would say to me now. Will I ever see her again?

But then, in this deepening darkness, bigger thoughts crowd my mind, hustling for position.

How did I end up here?

Will Joseph's family ever accept me?

Will my own family always be ashamed of me?

Did we really both see an angel?

Will my husband ever love me?

Who is this baby and what will he become?

Jesus looks so ordinary. So small and fragile.

So pure and helpless, yet... can I dare to believe that something bigger is going on here?

I have to.

It must be.

None of it makes sense. All I'm left with is trusting that God is bigger than this chaos. Bigger than this mess and confusion. Bigger than all I can see.

I have lost so many friends. No one wants to associate with me. Not that that makes any difference – I don't know anyone here anyway. I have no idea when I will get the chance to see any of my friends again. I know they were all whispering behind my back, saying God must have abandoned me, each one wondering what I did to get into this mess. But they all think they know exactly what I did.

And my family – I know they love me, but even my own mother couldn't hide the pity in her eyes when we said goodbye. My own vision was distorted with loss and tears but I could feel her shame. I sensed it in her touch, a little more reserved, like she was holding back.

And if my own family are struggling to accept this situation, how on earth can I expect Joseph's to be any different?

When we first dreamed of coming to Bethlehem, Joseph smiled as he talked about showing me off to his aunties, and how they would fuss over me and try to fatten me up ready for having a baby – one day, soon. His enthusiasm was infectious and I found myself swelling with expectation. I wanted to make him proud. I wanted to make my parents proud and now, now... well, that was before. Before the visits in the night and holy riddles. Before the call to have faith beyond all I could see or understand.

In the middle of all these questions, in the middle of all these uncertainties, there's Jesus. This little baby. Warm and soft, cooing and… screaming his head off and I have no idea what I need to do to keep him quiet.

Then there's the angel's words, 'Do not be afraid'. There's the witness of my cousin Elizabeth and her miracle son, John. Even though so much of it doesn't make sense, I've decided to trust in Yahweh, who is bigger than my confusion and doubts. Jehovah, who Abraham trusted with Isaac's life. Adonai, who Naomi remained faithful to, even when she lost so much.

I expected all this to be so different.

When I dreamed of our first home, it was filled with furniture and carvings lovingly crafted by a husband who cherished me. Not this cave on the outskirts of town, hidden away from disdainful eyes.

I didn't expect to be outcasts in a town Joseph had talked about with such fondness. This was supposed to be a new life, a new beginning and a fresh start. But what is there for us here?

I can see the pain in Joseph's face. I know he shares my sense of loss and isolation. In my darkest moments, I fear he is doubting his decision.

But these thoughts are fleeting. In the morning, I see his kind determination to protect us. To protect his son and love us both, even at such a great cost.

Given the way he is sticking by me, I can't really complain about the snoring.

Please stay near us, Yahweh. Please show us You are here. Please show me You will keep Your promises, even though this looks like such a mess. Keep us safe, Jehovah. Help me look after Jesus well, to be a good wife. To honour You, even though nothing is how I expected it to be.

*There is no historical evidence Joseph snored.

Faith amidst uncertainty

(Rachel)

'But Mary treasured up all these things and pondered them in her heart.' (Luke 2:19)

If you have the time: Luke 1:26–38

It was the end of 2009 – a year of watching Sam balance on the brink of death too many times. One evening I had responded to a cry from Tim, only to find him hovering over our eldest son, giving him mouth-to-mouth resuscitation as drips of lukewarm water soaked our bathroom floor.

It was nearly Christmas and the week after giving Sam CPR. I sat in our cold summerhouse at the bottom of the garden, nestled under a pile of blankets. Tinsel and lights filled the windows of our home, and I sat gripping a hot cup of tea in the relative darkness and began to pray.

I thought of Mary.

She was a vulnerable young woman who found herself in

a mess – engaged to marry a man while carrying a baby that wasn't his. She embarked on a scary and rough ride. When Mary gave birth to Jesus she was homeless, destitute and starting a marriage on the most difficult terms.

If I had been her, I would have felt abandoned by a God whom I had diligently served. Alone and scared, she must have felt forgotten and exiled. Those around her may have thought these hard-luck times were her own doing and demonstrated God's disapproval of her. I saw past the tinsel and tree, beyond the quaint, sterilised nativity, to a frightened and lost young woman struggling to understand what was happening to her.

Without the saintly glow or iconic pale blue headscarf, I could relate to Mary, her sense of confusion and uncertainty. My life was no reflection of what I had hoped or expected. I couldn't see purpose, rhyme, nor reason. Sam was living on the brink of death and our family edged along a tightrope of life-threatening epilepsy.

So often the whys and hows of life cannot be explained. In my little summerhouse, tucked away from the world, I chose to trudge down a road of trust and acceptance to hope and freedom, even when it didn't make sense. When our emotions fade, when logic does not bring satisfactory answers, sometimes all we are left with is a decision.

A choice to keep believing. A choice to trust.

A year before Sam was born (2004), I stood on my aunt and uncle's veranda in New Zealand. The faith I had grown up with had fallen away. I no longer had the feelings of devotion and relationship with God that I had once taken for granted. I remember listening to the Hillsong song, *With All I Am*: 'Jesus, I believe in you; Jesus, I belong to you'.[12] For me it was a sacred moment. Standing, looking at the neighbouring gardens, I chose to believe in Jesus.

Today, hearing that song still makes me cry. I will never forget that decision to have a faith bigger than what made sense or how I felt. This decision didn't mean I was now void of doubt; it actually meant I was determined to sit with my doubts, my fears and my fragile emotions, not whitewash them and pretend it was alright. But in the fear, confusion and uncertainty I clung to something bigger, determined to continue to stumble forward in any way I could.

In my summerhouse, back during Christmas 2009, I clung to that faith amidst uncertainty. I clung to the memory of that sacred moment. Then it dawned on me that if I only saw goodness in the easy times, I might just be missing out on something truly great.

For those looking at the life of Mary and the birth of Jesus, things might have seemed terribly messy – poorly planned and heartbreaking for all those involved. But what couldn't be seen by the human eye was that God was in fact doing His greatest work. His incarnation was real and dirty, messy and vulnerable. In that darkness and confusion, God was changing the history of the world and showing Himself to us in a more intimate way than ever before.

Can you recall a time you made a commitment to God?

It might be your baptism, the time you came to faith or maybe today is that first time.

If you feel able to, say or write a prayer. I began to write one out but realised it just showed all my own insecurities. So instead, in quiet, sit next to God – He's there. Talk to Him, tell Him your doubts and fears, and tell Him you want to trust Him anyway.

_____

_____

_____

_____

_____

_____

_____

_____

_____

Wrestling

(Rachel)

'Then the man said, "Your name will no longer be Jacob, but Israel, because you have struggled with God and with humans and have overcome."' (Genesis 32:28)

If you have the time: Genesis 32:22–31

This is where I tell you I'm a wrestler. Inspired by Big Daddy in the 80s, and several tons of cake and some back-breaking training later...

Sadly, I'm kidding. The only physical wrestling I do is rough and tumble with our boys, but I do find myself struggling in other ways.

Jacob's name was changed to Israel, which means 'God-wrestler'. I would be a bit concerned if God decided to change my name according to my behaviour. I might just end up being known as Chocoscoff, or simply SaltnVinegar.

Although Jacob's name isn't food related, I don't think it magnifies his finest hour. Jacob's behaviour was less than squeaky clean, and his journey to this point (and beyond) was brutal, bloody and devious. Jacob was known for trying to wheedle his way out of things. Yet God was with him and recognised his struggle.

To me it feels instinctive to try to avoid suffering and take the easy route out – the one that steers clear of any hand-to-hand combat. But, no matter how much I try to employ Jacob's tactics of softening the blow or side-stepping confrontation, I am frequently wrestled to the ground. When a challenging situation arises, our 'fight or flight' reflexes kick in.

Do we run for the hills or stick around and slog it out?

However, the drive to avoid suffering can in fact fuel fear. When we are persistently engineering our lives to avoid disappointments or challenges, we give credence to the voice of fear in our lives. By constantly relying on protective mechanisms, we close shop to the potential of living a full life.

The experience of grief may tempt us into avoiding love. The experience of failure might entice us into playing safe. As the parent of a child with a life-limiting condition, I look to the future and know it is going to get tricky. So, my choice is either to duck and dive, weave and shuffle, trying desperately to minimise the devastation; or I can stop and absorb what I'm feeling. Given that I don't know how long Sam will live, I want to wrestle every ounce of living from life.

Whatever brings us to the point of brokenness, whatever causes us to wrestle with God, whatever stretches us to our limit and beyond, the question we are left with is always, 'How will I respond?' Do we push it away, scream and run? Or do we press on, engage with it, wrestle with it, listen and learn?

By the very nature of Jesus, God lives in our world. He embraced our loss and grief, our fear and pain and made it His. That doesn't stop it hurting or being downright rubbish at times, but it does mean that our pain no longer needs to be wasted. When we get to the end of our rope, we find out what sustains us. We discover the Spirit who holds us. When all is lost, we can discover beauty that endures. It is in the wilderness that God does His best work. It may not be what you planned, but He is the God of the upcycle. He can take anything that is shattered or unwanted and make it His own.

We might end up walking with a limp, but sometimes it's right to wrestle with God and our circumstances. He can take the direst situations and nurture goodness from within them. When we abandon the pursuit of avoiding suffering, we can instead open our lives to the opportunities and gifts it holds.

DISH CLOTH MEDITATION

Get hold of a dish cloth.

Soak it in water.

Lift it out.

Feel how heavy the material feels in your hand as it drips excess water.

Concentrate on the fibres, unable to contain the water as it spills over your hands.

You could place it down on the side, full and seeping, allowing water to drain off the surface onto the floor – or you can take it in your hands and wring it out.

Twist the fabric between your fingers until you see your knuckles whiten.

Feel the ache and tiredness in your joints as you squeeze with all your strength.

Feel the discomfort of the fabric as friction burns in the palm of your hands. Wrestle the cloth; get all the water out if you can.

See the water pour through your fingers and hear the drips land on the surface below.

Feel the lightness of the cloth now.

Lay it out to dry.

What does God want you to wrestle?

What do you need to try to get every last drop out of?

Healing

(Tim)

> 'His disciples asked him, "Rabbi, who sinned, this man or his parents, that he was born blind?"
> "Neither this man nor his parents sinned," said Jesus'
> (John 9:2–3)

If you have the time: John 9:1–12

1 Samuel 16:7 is a Sunday school favourite: 'People look at the outward appearance, but the LORD looks on the heart.' It's linked to similar popular sayings such as 'never judge a book by its cover', 'beauty is only skin deep', and 'all that glitters is not gold'.

It was also the theme of a recent all-age service at our church. We looked at why God chose David above all his older, bigger, stronger brothers. It's an ongoing theme running through the Bible. We humans mistakenly pride physical or mental strength over the inner spiritual qualities that God treasures: perseverance, faith and love. One of the core attributes of our God is that He values us as His unique, beloved creations and not according to our physical or mental attributes.

Why then, when it comes to healing, are we obsessed with the physical and expect God to be too?

When Sam was ten weeks old, we stopped praying that his brain would be physically healed. An MRI scan confirmed he had severe and global brain damage. Up until that point, we and our church had been praying for and believing that Sam had escaped his traumatic first few weeks unscathed. The MRI scan was a watershed moment; a line in the sand. It was an answer to prayer and the answer was 'no'.

The expression 'watershed moment' comes from the geographical term describing the area of land that supplies water to one river. At the ridge of a mountain range, all the water falling on the ground at one side is supplying one river – but step over the ridge and the water drains to a completely different river. It might be hundreds of miles away, perhaps heading in the opposite direction. That one step over the watershed makes all the difference.

We stopped asking for Sam to be physically healed as we crossed a watershed of our own, partly due to feelings of loss, defeat and fatigue, but also because we had heard from God, loud and clear. He was saying 'no', but over time we came to realise He was not saying 'no' to healing, just 'no' to our *kind* of healing. We had to learn a whole new type of healing to be praying for; healing which was much more in line with God's priorities. The shock was that the healing had to take place in us, not Sam.

Sam has been the victim of a number of 'drive-by prayers' while enjoying a stroll in his wheelchair. 'Drive-by prayer' is the phrase we have coined to describe the experience of having a complete stranger, suddenly and without invitation, coming up to Sam, seeing that he is confined to a wheelchair, and spontaneously praying for him.

The last time this phenomenon occurred was during a visit to Salisbury cathedral. We were wandering around as a family, amazed by our surroundings. I was getting to grips with the history of the building and Rachel was soaking up the spirituality of the place (as usual). We were then spotted by a member of the clergy. Dressed in robes that signified her station, she suddenly approached and offered to pray for Sam. I was shocked enough to simply say 'yes', so she prayed and then went, leaving me a little bewildered.

As Rachel and I tried to untangle our feelings after the clergywoman had left, we realised that something was amiss. The very well-intentioned prayer had been entirely focused on Sam's physical appearance: a clearly disabled child in a wheelchair. However, in reality it was Rachel and I who needed prayer, and much more than Sam. She had focused on the outside, when God looks at the heart. Despite Sam's physical appearance he is very much spiritually whole, whereas I usually find myself in varying levels of spiritual brokenness.

If Sam is visiting a hospital, it would be understandable for a doctor to ask what they can do for him. As a doctor, I strive to help people with their physical or mental health, but have to admit I leave their spiritual needs largely unattended. But in a church situation, Sam is quite possibly the least needy person in the community or building. Sam has less work required on his soul to be more like Jesus than everyone else.

Surely healing from God's perspective is a bigger thing than our physical preconceptions of what looks or feels good; bigger than just postponing death for a few more years, or improving our sporting ability or our appearance, or our ability to pass exams. Not to belittle these very important things, but to redress the balance. If we employ a much deeper, kingdom-value-based view of healing, we might see healing as a spiritual transformation of our understanding of what is making us 'sick'. Taking this one step further: what if our physical or mental suffering is actually leading to our spiritual healing? And if God prioritises spiritual healing over physical, what are we expecting Him to do?

Those of us who live with chronic illness or disability may have already crossed that watershed to follow God's healing river away from our human preoccupation with the 'outward appearance' (though, naturally, we may also continue to ask for God's healing for life's physical sufferings). Wherever you are on your healing journey, be encouraged to follow the sweeping, undulating river of God's Spirit as He transforms you to be more of you in Him, inside and out.

RAISIN MEDITATION

Go to the kitchen and find a raisin.

Take a closer look at this tiny, dried grape.

Spend time examining it – get a magnifying glass if you need to. Observe its colour, its ridges and wrinkles, its peaks and valleys.

Don't rush. The more time you spend, the more you see.

It may be misshapen; mottled; irregular.

It may not be very pretty.

Once you feel you really know your raisin, pop it in your mouth and release the flavour.

Notice the sweetness, the distinctive flavour that reminds you of scones, Christmas cake, or maybe mince pies.

Experience this sensation as it fades from your mouth.

Consider how the joy and essence of that raisin has nothing to do with its physical appearance or attributes.

Know that God relishes, sees and loves you as so much more than what is on the outside.

Unanswered prayer

(Tim)

'*In the same way, the Spirit helps us in our weakness.
We do not know what we ought to pray for, but the Spirit
himself intercedes for us through wordless groans.*'
(Romans 8:26)

If you have the time: Acts 11:27–12:7

Before Sam was born, my faith in prayer had never really
been challenged. Things had largely gone my way, and that
which didn't could be easily explained. My faith had a degree
of immaturity. Then life happened, and I found the shape of
my faith didn't neatly marry with what I was experiencing.

It's important that our faith grows into maturity: just as
our understanding of the world at age six is quite different at
age 60, so should be our understanding of God. Sam's birth
was a faith-changing episode for me. I found in particular that
I had to reconsider my understanding of prayer.

In the months leading up to Sam's birth, I had got myself
into a pretty steady routine. Looking back (probably with

the heavily tinted glasses of retrospect) it all seemed bright, ordered and simple. We were recently settled in our new terraced house with its freshly stripped floorboards and small room set aside as a nursery. The house was about ten minutes' walk from the hospital, where I worked as a doctor in the department for care of the elderly. I walked those ten minutes in rain and shine – in the early hours following a nightshift, and in the dark nighttime trudge after a long day on call.

As I walked, I prayed, fresh with the hopes and dreams of married life with a child on the way, home making, and my career taking off. Even the hard days at work did little to dampen my expectant prayers. I prayed with each step that Rachel's pregnancy would continue to go well. I prayed that the birth would proceed as planned, and that our child would be well, whole, healthy. I prayed with confidence that even though I knew childbirth can be a difficult time for many, we would be OK. My prayers gave me confidence that we would continue to be blessed. I prayed every time I made that journey, with faith and perseverance.

Then life happened.

The pregnancy did not continue as expected. The birth did not go well. Despite my earnest praying, my son suffered catastrophic brain damage at some point before and also during his birth.

When we returned home from a stay in neonatal intensive care, I returned to work. As Rachel stayed at home, struggling to breastfeed, no longer able to comprehend what life was all about, I found myself making that exact same journey to work.

My feet hit the same pavement, the same bag on my back, the same houses passed. But nothing felt the same. The familiar rhythm of my journey led me back to a place of prayer, but as soon as the thought crossed my mind there were no words, only tears. Time and again I would walk back from work, crying the whole way, wondering if people would notice. I would try to sort out my snotty face before presenting myself as the strong husband for Rachel. Clearly, she could see I'd been crying. I remember coming home one day and all she said was, 'You look how I feel.'

There was anger at God, certainly. Also, bitter disappointment, disbelief and a sense of abandonment. There were also many questions.

What was the point of all those prayers?

Why would God let this happen in the face of my earnest praying when everyone else seems to have healthy children?

What difference would it really make if I never prayed again?

But mostly there was just emptiness and tears.

Maybe the apostles asked similar questions about James' death. It's reasonable to assume they prayed earnestly for his release, just as they did for Peter. But Peter was miraculously freed (Acts 12:7), and James died by the sword (Acts 12:2). The painful inconsistencies of prayer remain.

It took a long time for me to start praying again in any real way; even saying grace at mealtimes was a struggle. Thanking God for the chips and beans while overlooking the fact that He had let our son get brain damage was just too much. The words simply gathered like a dry ball in my throat, impossible to swallow.

The words did finally form over time, although I felt much less comfortable asking for things and perhaps less expectant that God would simply give me what I wanted. For me, this is still a work in progress. I know God wants to hear my prayers and my heart's desires, but I also know that no matter the outcome, if my prayers line me up with the heart of God, we are getting somewhere.

Looking back on it all now, I can see that as I trudged to work, heartbroken before God, my wordless sobs were my most real and wholehearted prayers. I thought I was too hurt to pray at all. Yet walking home with angry, bitter tears in my eyes, thinking that I had no words, were the times when I was at my most honest and vulnerable with God.

Try to sit in prayerful silence without expressing words.

Open the palms of your hands as an invitation to God's Spirit.

Simply breathe and know the anointing of God.

Allow the Holy Spirit to fill the quiet.

THE VIEW THROUGH MISCARRIAGE
Diane and Patrick's story (Patrick)

Diane and I always wanted to have a family, although we never really firmed up exactly how big. After our third child was born I'd assumed we were done, but Diane, who's from a family of five, was eager for another child. Although I wasn't too keen at first, I slowly warmed to the idea, especially as I saw how much it meant to Diane.

We found out we were pregnant a fourth time, and Diane was delighted. She later admitted she had been praying for God to either remove this desire from her heart or soften mine, and clearly God chose the latter. So I too became excited at the thought of a new addition to our family.

Then, when Diane was 13 weeks pregnant, she had some light bleeding. She wasn't too worried to start with as it had happened with our previous child, and everything had been fine – but this time was different. When Diane went to hospital, no heartbeat could be heard. She was told that our baby had stopped growing at nine weeks. We were no longer having a baby.

I wasn't with her at the time. Diane was devastated and could not speak. Her simple text said, 'Sorry babe.' I felt useless and guilty for initially not wanting this fourth child but also angry at God, wondering how He could let this happen.

Diane had to endure an operation to remove what the medics described as the 'products of conception' and she didn't want me to be with her. She felt numb and deeply upset. Her longed-for baby had been reduced to medical terminology. This wasn't a mass of cells – it was her baby, her future, her hope. She had believed this baby to be a precious gift from God.

Walking through the loss of miscarriage triggered a mixture of emotions for us both. Diane went from shock to deep sadness. She couldn't understand how God could finally answer her prayers for another child only to then take it away.

Throughout, my focus was on looking after Diane and I kept telling myself I had to be the strong one. I assumed that because she had carried our baby, suffered the miscarriage physically and then endured the resulting operation, she had more of a right to grieve. I measured up our sense of loss and decided hers was worse. I reasoned that because her pain was bigger, I should bury my hurt. Obviously, this wasn't exactly helpful.

While the experience was initially something we suffered individually, it soon brought us together as we had to announce the sad news to our family. We'd told the kids about the baby, who we sensed was a boy and decided to name Joel. For a while afterwards he was still very much part of our family.

Diane began praying again for God to take away the desire for another child, or to once again become pregnant. Finally, after two years, a successful pregnancy gave us our fourth child and second son.

The miscarriage opened us up and exposed how we grieve. We now recognise the need to face the pain we carry inside. Suppressing it is not helpful, even if you are the 'alpha male' of the family. We've also learned the hard lesson of opening up to others, even when it feels excruciatingly vulnerable. We need others as well as each other.

In 2018, Diane and I started a new charity called Kintsugi Hope. Through the experience of our miscarriage, and many other events, we were at the limits of our physical and emotional strength, brought quite literally to our knees. Our dream is that, through Kintsugi Hope, people going through times of trial and emotional turmoil for whatever reason can come to a safe place, be real and find God.

Diane and Patrick Regan

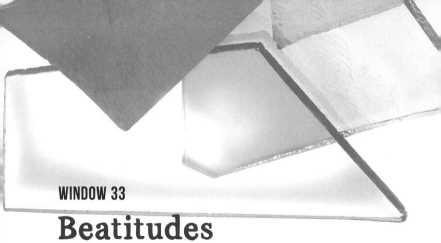

Beatitudes

(Rachel)

'Blessed are the poor in spirit,
for theirs is the kingdom of heaven.' (Matthew 5:3)

If you have the time: Luke 6:20–26

That morning, Jesus had people all over Him, vying for His attention and wanting to hear Him speak. As the heat of the day rose, He climbed above the crowds and pondered what His Father wanted Him to say.

His fame was growing. Maybe this man really was the Messiah. Maybe, unlike the men who had come before, He would be the one to deliver them into freedom. They were expectant of a revolution. They could smell change in the air. The day was hot and the ground dry. Layers of dust had already begun sticking under Jesus' sandals as He walked.

The disciples beamed at the growing popularity; at their presence in the middle of this insurrection. But as Jesus began to speak, His words cut through the murmur of expectation like a centurion's sword. Jesus spoke with tenderness and passion, complexity and simplicity. He began turning everything upside down and the people weren't happy. This isn't what they anticipated. This isn't what they came to hear. Where was the uprising? Where was the grand plan for opposition? Jesus spoke:

'You're blessed when you're at the end of your rope. With less of you there is more of God and his rule.

You're blessed when you feel you've lost what is most dear to you. Only then can you be embraced by the One most dear to you.

You're blessed when you're content with just who you are—no more, no less. That's the moment you find yourselves proud owners of everything that can't be bought.

You're blessed when you've worked up a good appetite for God. He's food and drink in the best meal you'll ever eat.

You're blessed when you care. At the moment of being 'care-full,' you find yourselves cared for.

You're blessed when you get your inside world—your mind and heart—put right. Then you can see God in the outside world.

You're blessed when you can show people how to cooperate instead of compete or fight. That's when you discover who you really are, and your place in God's family.

You're blessed when your commitment to God provokes persecution. The persecution drives you even deeper into God's kingdom.'

(Matthew 5:3–10, *The Message*)

I've always loved the Beatitudes, but I used to think they were Jesus' version of the booby prize; His passing glance to the 'less than', saying, 'Don't worry, you'll be OK. You'll be blessed too.' (Imagine being patted on the head.) But these days I can see they are so much more profound than that. Jesus knows that God's purpose, plan and power emanate through our brokenness. It is our shattered edges that form the best foundation for God's blessing – not for them to be miraculously fixed, but for each of us to find a deeper, more intense experience of life, God's values, and dependence on Him.

Think about these words and how they are deeply counter-intuitive and yet deeply true. When Jesus spoke, He reminded His listeners then, and us now, that being blessed is not found in the easy or nice but in the challenging and gritty. Our brokenness is where God penetrates our lives the most. We are most blessed in those places because God doesn't need a crowbar or hand grenade to break through. Our brokenness brings with it the openness and vulnerability needed for the transforming and redeeming power of Jesus to penetrate our lives in a richer way. These broken ways crack open our minds to see life in a new way – God's way.

When Jesus said, 'Blessed are the poor in spirit', He knew our best can be in our shattered, vulnerable and dependent state. Through our dependence on community we are blessed. Through the revelation that we are not in control, we surrender more deeply to God's unseen world. When we love others, we more keenly know God's love for us. When we are parched and dry, we crave God's Spirit to satisfy our thirst like spring rain on arid soil. This painful, broken place is a beautiful and bountiful opportunity for blessing.

Re-read those words of the Beatitudes three times.
  Let them sink in.
  Can you see how God has blessed you?
  Can you connect these blessings with your
brokenness?

_____

_____

_____

_____

_____

_____

_____

The Messiah
(Rachel)

'The people of Jerusalem and their rulers did not recognise Jesus, yet in condemning him they fulfilled the words of the prophets that are read every Sabbath.' (Acts 13:27)

If you have the time: Luke 4:16–30

Every Christmas, Christians around the world remember the nativity and life of Jesus. I marvel at the manger and the tenderness of God within it. Yet the undercurrent of my awe is tainted with an exasperation that the Jewish people of the day failed to see the Messiah when He was right in front of their eyes.

How on earth could they have been so blind?

Did they not see all the obvious signs?

They were so caught up with how they *imagined* the Messiah to be that they missed God walking among them. The Messiah was going to be their warrior king, their knight in shining armour. He would overcome the Romans and set them free – victorious. He was going to swoop in, transforming

Jewish history, establishing the nation of Israel, heralding an era of peace, and making their nation great once and for all.

As I rehear the Christmas story of a baby born into poverty, I gleefully proclaim the incarnate God coming not in a lavish fanfare as we might expect, but to the lowly, the broken and outcast. My attitude still bristles with contempt when I think that the religious leaders of Jesus' time missed what God was all about, even to the point of death on a cross.

But then I wonder if we are still behaving in exactly the same way. Today. Here. Now.

No one likes pain, and no one wants to see someone they love hurting. When life is hard and I'm swallowed up with grief, I want God to waltz in and take it all away. When I am consumed by difficulties and pain, I want my knight in shining armour to prove Himself by making it all better.

But if I look at the life of Jesus as a blueprint of the character of God, that is not how He works. That has never been how He operates.

I have a boy who thinks laundry belongs on the floor, and shoes wherever he took them off (actually, I have a husband with the same idea). When I tell my son to tidy his room, the response can vary – but he inevitably lands on the floor, disheartened and fed up. From the confines of his pants-books-and-toy-strewn den, I hear his echoing call: 'Will you help me?'

What he actually means is, 'Will you do it for me?'

In my stronger parenting moments, instead of stomping and grunting around the room and causing toys to thud heavily in trays and boxes, I sit on the floor with him and wait until he has the resolve to stand with me – then we get the job done together.

Isn't that what the whole of Scripture tells us God does?

I am yet to hear the story of a person's tricky, complex and challenging life being instantly fixed by God, who stepped in and changed all the difficult circumstances in a blink. All issues fixed, the only thing left to do is to glide through life like a 10/10 waltz on *Strictly Come Dancing*. The stories I know of tend to involve more hurt and tragedy, triumph and mercy, grace and a limitless amount of love. The more I see of God's character through Jesus' life, the more I come to terms with the fact that He is less likely to simply spring-clean my messy bedroom. Instead He sits on the floor with me until I'm ready to stand, and we both do the work together.

As I slowly help my son tidy his room, I wonder if I am still held hostage by rose-tinted religious views of God and how He operates. Maybe I could abandon my ideals of a Fairy-God-Father who shows up with His magic wand and fixes everything. What if I searched for the Jesus who is passionate for the shattered, and meets them in their brokenness? The Jesus who sought out the marginalised because God is powerful in our weakness; in the mess, the mire, the pain and dirt? As Ann Voskamp challenges us in her book *The Broken Way*: 'Maybe there's a Comforter who holds us gently in our brokenness.'[13]

God has always shown His love for us by being present in everything, while lovingly wanting to see us grow. Maybe it is time for me to stop waiting for the Messiah to fix everything around me. Instead, I could open myself to a different Messiah, the incarnate God, who arrived in our messy world longing to change my heart more than my circumstances.

God, help me to see You. To see Your hope, Your hands and Your presence, not just in the good parts of my life but especially in the hard and difficult parts. Instead of you transforming everything around me, I want to be transformed by You. Amen.

Communion

(Tim)

'And he took bread, gave thanks and broke it, and gave it to them, saying, "This is my body given for you; do this in remembrance of me."' (Luke 22:19)

If you have the time: 1 Corinthians 11:23–26

I'm not sure I should, but I find the paraphernalia surrounding Holy Communion quite amusing. The fancy cups and the linen dribble-wiper; the brass plate to hold the pre-broken Sainsbury's tiger bread. Most of all, the tiny cups many churches use, which look like miniature shot glasses but only ever contain Ribena. Then there's the gentle clatter as we all slot our glasses into the specially designed chairs with holes, having drained them in one unified, blackcurranty gulp. I think the reason it tickles me is that it seems so far removed from what Jesus was doing with His friends that Passover in the upper room over two thousand years ago.

The way I see it, we have sanitised, bleached, washed out, and neatly packaged Communion for easy consumption. We have made it fit in nicely with our quick-fix, fast-food, throw-away-and-start-again culture. I'm not sure it's right and I think we are missing out a great deal of what it has to offer – in particular, what it can teach us about being broken.

Communion is, at its core, a meal with friends and family around a table, sharing food with each other and, more importantly, sharing our lives. How often does your church celebrate Communion as part of a meal around a table, chatting about the ups and downs of life? Whenever we've done this, I have always felt more connected with my church family – as though I have glimpsed the heart of what Communion is all about. Communion in the context of community suddenly makes sense again.

However, it's so much more than *just* a meal with friends. The Passover meal is the illustration Jesus uses to explain His sacrifice and our deliverance. This meal, which had been celebrated for generations before Jesus and is still celebrated by Jews across the globe today, is a meal of remembering great suffering in slavery at the hands of the Egyptians, and of their ultimate freedom from that slavery. The whole family gathers, reclining around a table, with children playing a central role. The food served symbolises that time in slavery: bitter herbs, vegetables dipped in salt water like tears, lamb of the sacrifice, and charoset, a sweet paste to remember the mortar used in constructing Egyptian buildings. Four cups of wine are drunk, each representing a different aspect of God's promise to deliver Israel from Egypt while the flat (unleavened) bread is torn. It is in this context that Jesus utters His Jewish-tradition-shattering statement: 'this is *my* body… This is *my* blood' (Matthew 26:26–28, emphasis added).

Up until that point, the bread had been an illustration of

the escape from Egypt, the lamb demonstrated the sacrifice required for freedom from slavery, and the wine represented the promises of God. But in that room, Jesus changed the script. Instead, He effectively said, 'This meal, which we have celebrated for generations, remembering the sufferings and freedoms of our people, is now also about me. It's a demonstration of my suffering, my brokenness and also the freedom that will come from this.'

In her book *The Broken Way*, Ann Voskamp challenges us that transformation happens on the bed of pain, and it is in entering each other's suffering that we make our life an act of Communion. Communion is a reminder that brokenness is central to our walk with Jesus. It was through brokenness that God chose to show Himself through Jesus. It's a reminder that generations before us have experienced life's suffering. It's a recognition that we also experience life's 'bitter herbs'. Communion is the moment when, as a collective Church, we stand (or sit) together and acknowledge that we are all broken but united in our brokenness. Communion is not simply about fixing our broken pieces; it's about acknowledging that this is the pattern in which God chose to express His love to us: 'broken and given'.[14]

I think this is what God calls us into. As we pass on the broken bread, we symbolise sharing the tender, fragile parts of our lives as a loving sacrifice to God and one another. In the vulnerability of our broken edges, we find wholeness through the broken Christ.

Share a Communion meal with friends.

Next time you eat with your home group or church friends, sit around the table and share how shattered you feel.

Spend a few moments breaking bread and remember Jesus' brokenness for us.

Crown of thorns
(Tim)

'The soldiers twisted together a crown of thorns and put it on his head. They clothed him in a purple robe and went up to him again and again, saying, "Hail, king of the Jews!" And they slapped him in the face.' (John 19:2–3)

If you have the time: Isaiah 53:1–7

Crowns don't tend to be part of our everyday wardrobe. You'd probably get more than a few sideways looks if you did the Saturday morning supermarket shop with a regal crown on your head.

Crowns tend to be found either at the bottom of the dressing-up box, waiting patiently for Christmas and the eager Magi, or on the head of royalty. Even the queen reserves use of her crown for very occasional ceremonies (apparently, it's a bit cumbersome while out walking the corgis).

Crowns carry very special meaning: they indicate status; they denote 'highness'. Jesus, however, never chose to wear a crown. The crown He was given was thrust upon Him while

He stood before Pilate. It was an instrument of humiliation. The crown of thorns became a trigger for the crowds calling to crucify Him. It angered them as Pilate said, 'Here is your king' – the priests replying, 'We have no king but Caesar.'

The crown would surely have been agony for Jesus to wear, but it was not primarily a method of physical torture. It was part of a joke the Roman centurions cooked up – to dress Jesus as a cartoon king with a reed in one hand and a tatty purple cloak on His back, with the uncomfortable crown made from a thorny bush found by the roadside. They were saying, 'Look at this wreck of a man. He thinks he is the "King of the Jews"!'

However, the joke was catastrophically misjudged. Not because they had got it so wrong, but because they had got it so right. They had so badly misunderstood the character of Jesus that they failed to see that the dressing-up clothes they used to mock Him actually represented Him perfectly. This was no ordinary king with a plush, fur-lined cloak, jewel-encrusted staff and golden crown.

This is Jesus, the humble King, the servant King.

This King is the King of sacrifice, the King of suffering.

Reflect on Philippians 2:5–8:

'In your relationships with one another, have the
same mindset as Christ Jesus:
who, being in very nature God,
did not consider equality with God something to be
used to his own advantage;
rather, he made himself nothing
by taking the very nature of a servant,
being made in human likeness.
And being found in appearance as a man,
he humbled himself
by becoming obedient to death –
even death on a cross!'

THE VIEW FROM RETIREMENT
Norman and Jan's story

Norman

How lovely it was to get away in our wee caravan, just the two of us. After the obligatory levelling, getting the gas, electric and water connected as well as the awning erected, we sat down with a deep sigh and a nice hot drink.

We began to dream of my impending retirement when the rush and stress would be lifted from us, along with the endless expectations of others upon our time. After a very short time, however, it dawned on us that we were not on the same page. In fact, what Jan was looking for in retirement was very different to my own expectations. To be honest, the next few days together did not bring much resolution. The most peaceful times were when we decided not to talk about the 'elephant in the caravan'.

We are not one of those couples who never argue, but it was a real challenge to discover that something we were both looking forward to was creating so much tension. One of the biggest barriers to us communicating well with each other was fear. From my teenage years, I have known a calling to serve God. My fear in retirement was that I would lose something at the core and essence of my life. My identity is firmly established in Jesus, but that has always expressed itself in a tangible ministry. Who and what would I be without the ability to live out my ministry?

Jan

For me, the fear was very different but just as real. For 45 years I have been married to a pastor and minister – and even when Norman was a full-time teacher, the calling he felt on his life determined where we lived and what we did. Everything was a joint decision but it didn't come without sacrifice. For years I cared for our children when Norman was away on ministry. Even as empty-nesters, I have prepared our meals – many of which are hurriedly eaten so that Norman can rush off to spend time with other people in need.

Norman's retirement heralded for me a time when 'us' and 'time together' would be top of the agenda. My fear, however, was fuelled by hearing of friends who had retired in good health only to find out soon after that illness, dementia or death would rob them of their hopes and dreams.

I now recognise that we were both struggling to hear each other's heart. Both of us tried to say the right thing. Norman tried to reassure me that he really *was* looking forward to having more quality time together, while I tried to make it clear that I wanted our service to God to continue to flow out of love for Him and each other. You'd think that after nearly half a century together we'd know each other's hearts well enough – but it's not always that easy.

The story so far…

Nine months into retirement, we are not pretending it has been plain sailing but we are doing well. God graciously continues to shape and mould us, as He often does, through each other. Norman has taken on a role working two days a week and we are taking the next step, approaching this season with curiosity and openness to all that might be in store, even though it is unlikely to be what either of us expected.

The Bible is full of how God has used disagreements between people, even spouses, to further His kingdom: Abraham and Sarah, Moses and Zipporah, David and Abigail... the list could go on. God does not ask us to gloss over our differences or pretend they are not there, but He says love is bigger than fear and insecurities.

'There is no fear in love. But perfect love drives out fear'
(1 John 4:18)

Despite the future looking different to what we both expected – despite our differences and hesitations – the heroes of faith we see throughout the Bible and history show us that it doesn't matter how long we have been together, there is always so much we can learn about ourselves and God through each other.

Norman and Jan Hooks

Being present
(Rachel)

*'There is a time for everything,
and a season for every activity under the heavens'*
(Ecclesiastes 3:1)

If you have the time: Ecclesiastes 3:1–8

I can be happily beavering around the house, shaking laundry, discovering rotten fruit under the sofa and throwing shoes in the porch, while a deluge of thoughts race through my mind at a hundred miles an hour. It might be something Tim said that morning that really ticked me off, or a really funny blog I want to craft. So often my brain can be consumed by an internal monologue that drowns out all my other senses. I don't notice the smell of the clothing, fruit or shoes. The sound of my feet on our wooden floor is barely noticeable because I'm thinking about the conversation I have just had or a witty comeback I should have responded with. I don't feel the water between my fingers as I wipe the kitchen surface because I'm writing a shopping list in my head.

It seems I spend more time in the past and future rather than actually being present. Here and now has stopped being anything concrete, and the present has become an untethered entity; wistful and hazy, always just out of reach.

I used to be so much worse (just ask Tim). I recall one lovely camping holiday we spent in the New Forest when we were dating. I was tearfully disappointed by the fact that Tim had yet to ask me to marry him. We were sitting up a tree, waiting for dusk to fall and deer to emerge from the twilight forest, when I decided this was the perfect time to talk about our future (again). Mostly I thought it was the perfect time to discuss Tim's tardiness and lack of willingness for us to be engaged. He was adamant he wanted to marry me, but just not now, not yet. I suspect he was also pretty perturbed by the fact my gentle (OK, hysterical) weeping might hinder him watching the emerging wildlife.

Not that it was right for Tim to make me wait so long before we got engaged (at the ripe old age of 20 and 22) but, in this instance at least, my obsession with the future totally ruined that evening up a tree – for both of us.

When Sam was born, my innate ability to spend hours fantasising about the days, weeks and years ahead came to an abrupt end. I could no longer see my future. I had no dreams that could contain my current scenario. I had no versions of my life where my situation made sense. So then I spent a lot of time stewing over the past. Remembering what could, should and ought to have happened but didn't, changing our lives forever.

With time and healing, I have slowly found the courage to abandon spending so much time in the past (most of the time). Letting go of everything that happened, abandoning the *what if* world for the hologram it is (Window 18). Today, my mind occasionally wanders to the future but not often. I still can't imagine Sam in four years' time, or what life might be like without him. With the past and future out of bounds, I am living much more in the present.

When I look around at what is happening, here and now, I am tempted to frame life as good or bad, rough or smooth, godly or evil. But I am profoundly comforted that the birth, life and death of Jesus demonstrates how everything is within the grasp of godliness. The ordinary and the extra-ordinary. The holy and bitter. The triumphant and broken. All of it can be held in the hands of God and His holiness.

In the book of Ecclesiastes we are challenged by the idea that there is a time for everything. All that we are living at this moment has a time and place:

> 'There is a time for everything,
> and a season for every activity under the heavens:
> a time to be born and a time to die,
> a time to plant and a time to uproot,
> a time to kill and a time to heal,
> a time to tear down and a time to build,
> a time to weep and a time to laugh,
> a time to mourn and a time to dance,
> a time to scatter stones and a time to gather them,
> a time to embrace and a time to refrain from embracing,
> a time to search and a time to give up,
> a time to keep and a time to throw away,
> a time to tear and a time to mend,
> a time to be silent and a time to speak,
> a time to love and a time to hate,
> a time for war and a time for peace.'

(Ecclesiastes 3:1–8)

We could learn a lot from Brother Lawrence, a sixteenth-century monk. In his wonderful book, *The Practice of the Presence of God*, Brother Lawrence shares how he thought thinking, praying and contemplating were the essence of a holy life. But when he joined the monastery, he discovered communion didn't stop when he started work. Rather, he found a way of working that meant his menial duties heightened his experience of God's presence.

Instead of stopping your busyness to be with God, embrace practising the presence of God as you go about your day.

As you 'do' living today, whatever that means, be mindful of God's presence and Spirit. In every move, every breath, every word and every action, consciously bring to mind God's Spirit in, around and through everything in this time and in this place.

Acceptance

(Rachel)

'The LORD is my shepherd, I shall not want.'
(Psalm 23:1, NKJV)

If you have the time: Philippians 4:10–19

I spent a long time believing that when the psalmist wrote, 'The LORD is my shepherd, I shall not want', he must have already had everything he wanted. It was a prayer of testimony to God's provision. But one day Tim had spent some time with God (in the bath, as usual) and shared with me how he was looking at that scripture differently. Rather than 'not wanting' being a declaration of abundance, the psalmist's source of peace came from arriving at a place where he was able to do away with 'wanting'.

The underlying theme of my memoir, *The Skies I'm Under*, traces this switch from seeking deliverance to finding contentment. This is what I wrote:

'I wanted to press past the pain of circumstances into contentment. Life tasted sweeter when I was no longer struggling against the circumstances of life. With the passing of time, I stopped focusing on the pavement in front of me, lifted my head and prayed differently. I stopped wanting the weather to change or the view to be different. Instead I prepared to dress more appropriately and appreciate where I was. I began to learn to love the skies I was under.'[15]

But, much like grief, I don't think acceptance is a linear path. One minute I can feel satisfied and content – then the happiness of a toddler splashing their bright red wellies in a puddle will crack open my heart with the realisation that Sam will never experience such a simple pleasure. In a second, my emotions lie like shattered debris at my feet.

Days containing unexpected and uninvited heartache cause me to make a complete U-turn. I time-warp backwards down my own 'road to recovery' until I am emotionally exactly where I was the day after Sam was born. The grief and regret are all too familiar and easy to put back on. But with the passing of time my recovery quickens, and after a prescription of chocolate and trashy TV my soul is soothed and I am once again able to see the blessings around me.

A large part of my own journey of acceptance revolved around my vision of myself. Since Sam had been born, I worried what people thought when they saw me. I would catch my reflection as sunlight glinted on the paintwork of a passing car. My heart would skip a beat at seeing myself pushing a child in a bright orange wheelchair as I wondered, *How did this happen? What must people be thinking?* But that too thawed with time. Initially, I avoided Facebook and contacting old friends because I recoiled from their sympathy and misconceptions. Then, like a recovering addict, I became confident in saying, 'My name is Rachel and my son is severely disabled.'

Today, although Sam does not define me, I am proud of the person he has helped me become (you would not believe the effort it took to write that). Sam's life and disabilities have formed my thinking and perspective. I have adapted to our new 'normal', but I doubt I will ever fully accept the limitations and pain in Sam's life.

There is a lot I still do not understand and struggle to accept, but I live in hope that God is participating in this messy world with me. In doing so I choose to recognise the freedom that arises from accepting my circumstances, not an illusion of freedom dependent on me escaping them.

ACCEPTANCE MEDITATION

Find some time and a quiet room.

Stand if you can, knees slightly bent, feet apart. Support your weight evenly and comfortably.

Close your eyes and wait.

Notice your breath rising and falling, filling and releasing.

Notice the feel of your feet on the ground, your limbs supporting your weight.

Over time you will feel minor discomforts.

A muscle might ache a little; a tendon complains; your feet feel the pressure.

See if you can choose to stay still. Resist the temptation to fix it.

Resist the temptation to chase after comfort.

Resist the temptation to make it go away but simply notice it, observe the discomfort and accept it.

Notice that often as you accept it, it fades away and you can return to stillness.

Every mile matters

(Rachel)

'And we know that in all things God works for the good of those who love him, who have been called according to his purpose.' (Romans 8:28)

If you have the time: Romans 8:16–30

I attempt to run regularly. However, I reserve the right to stomp around the house like a tantruming toddler beforehand and scowl at anyone (Tim) who tries to encourage me. The bit I dislike the most about running is the beginning, the middle and the end. A sure-fire way to hasten a decline in my mood is for me to be overtaken while out running. Tim likes to point out that now I'm 'the other side of 40', a six-foot-tall, 20-year-old athlete may well be faster than me, but what does he know? I do, however, enjoy arriving home again.

Predominantly it is my love for crisps and chocolate fudge brownies that fuels my passion for running. So, when I really want to indulge the eating, I counter it by entering a marathon. The training needed six weeks before a marathon race is tough, mostly because it is so time-consuming. Every mile matters. When I come back from a slow, sluggish and painful training run, I can at least take comfort from the fact that every mile contributes to my overall fitness on race day.

Even the slow runs.

Even the cut-short runs.

Even the painful and demoralising runs.

They all count.

And that is true for every aspect of our lives. It all counts. None of it is wasted. None of it is futile. It might be painful. It might not be how God intended it. It definitely might not be what I dreamed of, but whatever occurs, God can make it count.

The soundtrack to my life for a while was Nichole Nordeman's album *Every Mile Mattered*.[16] There are several tracks on that album that have ministered to me, but one in particular is the title track.

In the song, Nichole wants to highlight the darker, harder roads she endured, recognising that God has used every step and every mile to mould and lead her into being the person she is today. I'd really encourage you to listen to it if you can.

Most people have heard of post-traumatic stress, but there is also such a thing as post-traumatic growth. Post-traumatic growth describes positive change that comes as a result of a traumatic experience. It isn't about returning to life as it was before but an evolution in thinking and relating to the world, which happens through a life-changing experience. It doesn't suggest all aspects of life will be better or easier, but rather a process of deep and meaningful personal transformation. Post-traumatic growth is simply a way of labelling what happens when the shattered, vulnerable places of our lives are the catalyst for change. It sounds so counter-intuitive and yet so obvious too.

Have you ever seen a white bluebell? Apparently, they do exist (though I didn't notice a white native bluebell until Tim pointed it out). There is a theory that while the bluebell bulb is developing and splitting underground, it is traumatised in some way. The trauma has caused a mutation, changing the bulb forever. When the flower then opens the following spring, instead of blue it appears perfectly white. It might look out of place, but for me, a white bluebell standing in a sea of blue looks perfectly wonderful. The changes endured by the bluebell mattered. Its history matters and has brought about lasting, beautiful change.

Maybe it is disruption that creates the fertile ground needed to nurture something new, unexpected and beautiful. When planting a harvest, the soil needs breaking up. It needs to be ploughed, dug over, sifted through and exposed. There may be a fallow period which feels hollow and void, but each step of our journey matters. It is the tilled ground that becomes ready to accept seeds to be sown. Each phase, each step, each aspect of our journey is not wasted but contributes to bringing us to this point.

I have heard Romans 8:28 used to support an idea that only good things happen to those who serve God. But I love this verse because I believe it says in everything – every mile, every tear, every hurdle, every experience – God transforms, renews and redeems. He is moulding, nurturing and breathing good into everything. Look up – it is happening now! Wherever you are, right at this minute, new shoots are peeking through the earth's crust, fertilised by your years of history. Like the bluebell, it may not be the colour you expected, but this place is bursting with potential, hope and unexpectedly spectacular blossom.

Go back and look at what you wrote in Window 2
– the defining moments of your life.

Think about these times more deeply, and reflect on what you've read in these pages.

What tender shoots can you see?

What growth can you nurture?

_____

_____

_____

_____

_____

_____

_____

_____

_____

_____

Nothing can separate

(Rachel)

'For I am convinced that neither death nor life, neither angels nor demons, neither the present nor the future, nor any powers, neither height nor depth, nor anything else in all creation, will be able to separate us from the love of God that is in Christ Jesus our Lord.' (Romans 8:38–39)

If you have the time: Romans 8:31–39

The real-life stories we have shared in this devotional show the depth and breadth of tragedy, hope, love, trials and unmet dreams we might have to take in our stride.

People of great faith and no faith – stories of divorce, death, doubt, pain and brokenness – all come together to create the tapestry of humanity. And holding it all together is love – God's love for us. Whether or not we can feel it or even want to acknowledge it, the greatest assurance we are given in Scripture is the promise that everything is held together by the power of God's love.

We see His love in the beauty of creation – the wild,

untamable, unruly beauty that continues to astound and baffle scientists every day. We glimpse the tenderness and complexity of God's love in the birth of Jesus – in God choosing to become incarnate in the humblest and messiest of ways, through a young refugee couple, alone and on the run. We see the unconditional nature of God's love in Jesus' teachings as He sat on a mountainside and blew the minds of His listeners, describing the upside-down kingdom of God – stretching them, challenging them, pulling apart all they thought they knew as truth. Jesus repeatedly, clearly and passionately set out God's stall for loving and honouring the broken and often forgotten. He pursued the sinners and sought the lost. Those who were sick, unclean and deemed untouchable.

Then we see it on the cross. God loves us enough to have died for us before we loved Him. That is the message of the gospel. That is the transforming hope of Jesus. Whether we see it or not, whether we live in the light of its truth or struggle to know it, God loves us. He is for us. That truth isn't dependent upon saying a few magic words. It isn't dependent upon our behaviour or the depth of our faith. It is the nature and being of God.

Jesus' call to us is this:

'love one another. As I have loved you, so you must love one another. By this everyone will know that you are my disciples, if you love one another.'

(John 13:34–35)

If Jesus was teaching us in our town and on our streets, would He be turning the tables on the churches for not opening their doors to the homeless, excluded and displaced? Would He be rallying against us for not speaking up for refugees; the oppressed at home and abroad? Would He be challenging us that since His love is big enough, why isn't ours?

When we are shattered by the challenges and heartbreak of life, the fundamental truth of God's love can feel shaken to the core. We wonder how He could possibly love us and let bad things happen. Our need to understand and make sense of it all dwarfs the seed of truth that we are created, loved, and have a purpose. Nothing in this book really gives a satisfactory answer to unanswered prayer. Nothing can explain suffering in a way that can satisfy a shattered heart. It remains a paradox that requires our faith and our hope. We are left with doubts and unanswered questions. We are still left living a life we didn't plan.

But with the truth that God's love is bigger than all of this, we are living with an invitation to live through our brokenness in the healing power of His love. Through Jesus' birth, teaching and death on the cross, God showed us in no uncertain terms that He deals in the shattered parts of our lives. His business is in the broken. He cares for the hurting. Our incarnate God shows us that it is through our brokenness that He invites us into wholehearted living, not in spite of it. This reality should not surprise us – it was the experience of Moses, David, Naomi, Job, Esther and Jesus. It is our story and the story of many of our contemporaries. It is the reality of living a fragile life in a broken world with a loving God.

We are called to live as God showed us through Jesus: to enter the mess and bring God's holiness, grace, love, perseverance and peace. It is still hard and it still hurts. That truth is not dampened because it is part of our story.

This is our story.

Our story of heartbreak and love.

A story of our shattered lives living alongside one another in love, allowing our brokenness to create a wholehearted life. The fragile, vulnerable edges can break open our relationships to be transformed by the brokenness of Christ on the cross.

Take heart that as you continue to walk this life, you do so knowing that this broken way is God's way; that our shattered selves are held together by the unchanging promise of His love, which gives us hope that in God, nothing is wasted.

Flick back through this book – what has stood out the most for you?

Take a moment of quiet and write down what you think God might be saying to you now.

_____

_____

_____

_____

_____

_____

_____

_____

_____

AFTERWORD

'Then I saw "a new heaven and a new earth," for the first heaven and the first earth had passed away' (Revelation 21:1)

God isn't in the business of going back but going forward.

There will be a new heaven and new earth – not a patched up, repaired old earth. Something beautiful, resplendent and unique will be forged. Like creating a beautiful stained glass window from shards of glass, God the creator will scoop up the broken pieces of our lives to make something colourful, captivating and new.

As you move on from here, we pray that you may know the love of God.

We pray that as you examine the shattered pieces of your life, you resist the temptation to try to put them back together the way they were.

We pray you find a tribe to walk with you.

We pray that in the broken edges of your life you notice how each striking fragment of tainted glass can be crafted together into a new spectacular stained glass window of life, where God's light shines through, scattering colour and beauty wherever you go.

ACKNOWLEDGEMENTS

All the mistakes in this book are ours and all the good bits were probably the influence of someone else. There are many people to thank for getting ink on paper.

All our dear friends who bravely shared their stories: Hannah, Jay, Rachel, Dan, Patrick, Diane, John, Alex, Emma, Sahar, Mohammad, Jan and Norman (our walking-talking Bible reference). Our parents (Norman and Jan, David and Janine) who support us in many ways – in particular David, who has provided constant encouragement while himself caring for Tim's mum. Grandma Doreen, thanks for being an extra special bonus grandma for our kids. Patrick and Diane Regan for being an inspiration and introducing us to Lynette and CWR. Bex at CWR for your enthusiasm and hard work through a traumatic time. The infamous Beans Club, Belle Vue Baptist Church, Beer Club, the Duprees, and our family of carers who make life possible: Lucy, Bex, Tracy, Sylvia, Dorrion, Natalia, Pauline, Christina, Karen, Ellie, Helen, Martina and Laura. Thanks to our three wonderful boys for the wealth of material that makes up this book.

And last but not least, all the luxuries we take for granted but which sustain us through life: crisps and hummus, chocolate, beer, Tim's new chainsaw, Rachel's hot water bottle and most importantly, sleep.

ENDNOTES

[1] Brené Brown, *Rising Strong* (London: Vermillion, 2015) p41

[2] *The Greatest Showman* dir. Michael Gracey (20th Century Fox: 2017)

[3] Pete Greig, *God on Mute: Engaging the Silence of Unanswered Prayer* (Eastbourne, UK: Kingsway Publications, 2007) p127

[4] Glennon Doyle, *Love Warrior: A Memoir* (London: Two Roads, 2017)

[5] Ann Voskamp, *The Broken Way* (Grand Rapids, MI, USA: Zondervan, 2016) p176

[6] Rachel Gardner, *Girl Deconstruction Project* (London: Hodder and Stoughton, 2018) p167

[7] Brené Brown, *Daring Greatly* (New York, NY, USA: Penguin Life, 2015) p69

[8] Glennon Doyle, *Love Warrior: A Memoir* (London: Two Roads, 2017)

[9] Barbara Brown Taylor, *Learning to Walk in the Dark* (New York, NY, USA: HarperCollins, 2014) p57

[10] Steve Peters, *The Chimp Paradox: The Mind Management Programme for Confidence, Success and Happiness* (London: Vermillion, 2012)

[11] Hillsong United, 'Take All of Me', *More than Life* (Hillsong Music and Resources LLC, 2004)

[12] Hillsong Worship, 'With All I Am', *For All You've Done* (Hillsong Music and Resources LLC, 2004)

[13] Ann Voskamp, *The Broken Way* (Grand Rapids, MI, USA: Zondervan, 2016) p75

[14] Ann Voskamp, *The Broken Way* (Grand Rapids, MI, USA: Zondervan, 2016) p172

[15] Rachel Wright, *The Skies I'm Under* (Great Britain: Born at the Right Time Publishing, 2017) p78

[16] Nichole Nordeman, *Every Mile Mattered* (Capitol Christian Music Group, 2017)

BOOKS WE'VE FOUND HELPFUL

(Mostly read by Rachel, as Tim prefers to read books about wood and/or the woods)

Karen Bowler, *Everything Happens for a Reason: And Other Lies I've Loved* (London: SPCK, 2018)

Brené Brown, *Braving the Wilderness* (London: Vermillion, 2017)

Brené Brown, *Daring Greatly* (New York, NY, USA: Penguin Life, 2015)

Brené Brown, *Rising Strong* (London: Vermillion, 2015)

Barbara Brown Taylor, *Learning to Walk in the Dark* (New York, NY, USA: HarperCollins, 2014)

Glennon Doyle, *Love Warrior: A Memoir* (London: Two Roads, 2017)

Rob Frost, *The Essence Course* (Eastbourne, UK: Kingsway Publications, 2002)

Rachel Gardner, *Girl Deconstruction Project* (London: Hodder and Stoughton, 2018)

Pete Greig, *God on Mute: Engaging the Silence of Unanswered Prayer* (Eastbourne, UK: Kingsway Publications, 2007)

Jen Hatmaker, *Of Mess and Moxie* (Nashville, TN, USA: Yates and Yates, 2017)

Krish Kandiah, *Paradoxology* (London: Hodder & Stoughton, 2014)

Brother Lawrence, *The Practice of the Presence of God* (London: Hodder Classics, 2009)

Lars Mytting, *Norwegian Wood: Chopping, Stacking and Drying Wood the Scandinavian Way* (London: MacLehose Press, 2015) – a special recommendation from Tim

Shauna Neiquist, *Bitter Sweet* (Grand Rapids, MI, USA: Zondervan, 2010)

Shauna Neiquist, *Present Over Perfect* (Grand Rapids, MI, USA: Zondervan, 2016)

Patrick Regan, *Honesty Over Silence* (Farnham: CWR, 2018)

Patrick Regan, *When Faith Gets Shaken* (London: Monarch Books, 2015)

Richard Rohr, *Falling Upward* (London: SPCK, 2012)

Sheryl Sandberg and Adam Grant, *Option B: Facing Adversity, Building Resilience, and Finding Joy* (London: Penguin Random House UK, 2017)

Jo Saxton, *The Dream of You* (London: Monarch Books, 2018)

Williams, Richards and Whitton, *I'm Not Supposed To Feel Like This: A Christian self-help approach to depression and anxiety* (London: Hodder & Stoughton, 2002)

Ann Voskamp, *One Thousand Gifts* (Grand Rapids, MI, USA: Zondervan, 2011)

Ann Voskamp, *The Broken Way* (Grand Rapids, MI, USA: Zondervan, 2016)

Rachel Wright, *The Skies I'm Under* (Great Britain: Born at the Right Time Publishing, 2015)

Wm Paul Young, *The Shack* (London: Hachette UK, 2008)

Courses and seminars

Waverley Abbey College

Publishing and media

Conference facilities

Transforming lives

CWR's vision is to enable people to experience personal transformation through applying God's Word to their lives and relationships.

Our Bible-based training and resources help people around the world to:
• Grow in their walk with God
• Understand and apply Scripture to their lives
• Resource themselves and their church
• Develop pastoral care and counselling skills
• Train for leadership
• Strengthen relationships, marriage and family life and much more.

Our insightful writers provide daily Bible reading notes and other resources for all ages, and our experienced course designers and presenters have gained an international reputation for excellence and effectiveness.

CWR's Training and Conference Centre in Surrey, England, provides excellent facilities in idyllic settings – ideal for both learning and spiritual refreshment.

CWR Applying God's Word to everyday life and relationships

CWR, Waverley Abbey House,
Waverley Lane, Farnham,
Surrey GU9 8EP, UK

Telephone: **+44 (0)1252 784700**
Email: **info@cwr.org.uk**
Website: **www.cwr.org.uk**

Registered Charity No. 294387
Company Registration No. 1990308